MW00390504

SHOE DESIGN

daab

Introduction   8

INTRODUCTION

In Shoe Design we want to show the great variety of creativity found in footwear design today. From designers continuing the tradition of elegant and more classical styles, to others exploring the experimental thereby changing our perception of the notion of footwear altogether. From bespoke and uniquely individual products to futuristically engineered concepts, shoe design can be interesting and challenging whilst retaining a sense of desirability.

Shoes have been a crucial part of the wardrobe throughout history. Starting with the practical need to protect from the elements, shoes quickly took on decoration and individual forms. The variety of footwear and constructions have developed dramatically throughout history and across many different cultures.

Footwear and accessories is now one of the most lucrative and important facets of today's fashion industry. Designers are paying more attention to accessories than ever before and consumer confidence has been steadily growing with a broader variety of desirable products available. Accessories are an easy-access route into a designer's vision and hold a gripping fascination for both women and men. We now have magazines, trade shows, trend analysis groups, blogs, books, fetishists and courses all dedicated to footwear.

Footwear design has recently gone through a renaissance as a creative field. New ideas are emerging with boundaries being pushed and new creative levels reached. Look to the latest catwalk shows and you can see why some of these extreme looks get the most press coverage; the focus is back on shoes.

In this book we want to show designers that have a unique identity regardless of commerciality, and a strong voice of their own, current trends aside. Not all are strictly shoe designers, but it is equally important to include the view of those that have not come from a footwear background as it is to feature those that have been in it for years. We have included global designers from various geographical and cultural backgrounds, but all share one common interest; a passion for shoes.

Mit dem vorliegenden Buch Shoe Design möchten wir die große Vielfalt an Kreativität zeigen, durch die sich das Schuhdesign von heute auszeichnet. Von Designern, die die Tradition eleganter und eher klassischer Modelle fortschreiben, zu denen, die sich dem Experimentellen verschrieben haben und unsere Vorstellung von Schuhen gänzlich auf den Kopf stellen. Von maßgeschneiderten und einzigartig individuellen Produkten zu futuristisch konstruierten Konzepten – Schuhdesign kann interessant und faszinierend sein und das Gefühl von etwas Begehrenswertem bewahren.

Im Laufe der Geschichte ist Schuhen bei der Bekleidung stets eine sehr wichtige Rolle zugekommen. Zunächst stand die praktische Notwendigkeit, sich vor den Elementen zu schützen, im Vordergrund, aber schnell wurden Schuhe geschmückt und erhielten individuelle Formen. Die Mannigfaltigkeit an Schuhen und Modellen hat sich im Laufe der Jahrhunderte und durch verschiedene Kulturen hindurch ganz erheblich entwickelt.

Schuhe und Accessoires stellen heute einen der lukrativsten und wichtigsten Bereiche der Modeindustrie dar. Designer legen heutzutage mehr denn je Wert auf Accessoires, und das Vertrauen der Kunden wächst stetig in Abhängigkeit zur größer werdenden Palette an verfügbaren begehrenswerten Produkten. Accessoires bieten einen leichten Zugang zu Vorstellung und Konzept eines Designers, und sie üben sowohl auf Frauen als auch auf Männer eine packende Faszination aus. Heute gibt es Zeitschriften, Fachmessen, Trendanalysen, Blogs, Bücher, Fetischisten und Kurse – alles dreht sich um Schuhe.

Als kreatives Feld hat Schuhdesign vor kurzem eine Renaissance erlebt. Neue Ideen tauchen auf, Grenzen werden verschoben, neue Levels an Kreativität erreicht. Schaut man sich die jüngsten Laufstegshows an, wird klar, warum einige dieser extremen Looks die Berichterstattung in den Medien dominieren – Schuhe stehen wieder im Mittelpunkt.

In dem vorliegenden Buch möchten wir Designer vorstellen, die sich, unabhängig von kommerziellen Aspekten, durch eine einzigartige Identität auszeichnen, die herrschende Trends ignorieren und stattdessen ihre eigene überzeugende Auffassung präsentieren. Streng genommen sind nicht alle von ihnen Schuhdesigner, aber es ist uns wichtig, sowohl die Sicht derjenigen einzubeziehen, die nicht aus der Schuhbranche kommen, als auch der Personen, die seit Jahren in diesem Bereich tätig sind. Wir haben eine Sammlung an Designern aus der ganzen Welt zusammengestellt, mit verschiedenen geographischen und kulturellen Backgrounds. Alle aber eint ein gemeinsames Interesse: die Leidenschaft für Schuhe.

En Diseño de Zapatos queremos mostrar la enorme riqueza creativa presente en el diseño del calzado actual. Desde diseñadores que se adhieren a la tradición de unos estilos elegantes y más clásicos, a otros que exploran lo experimental y que transforman por completo nuestra percepción del concepto de calzado. Desde productos confeccionados a medida o plenamente individualizados, pasando por conceptos de ingeniería futurista, el diseño de zapatos puede resultar interesante y desafiante, y al mismo tiempo conservar una esencia ligada al deseo.

A lo largo de la historia, los zapatos siempre han ocupado un lugar crucial en el vestuario. Creados en primera instancia por la necesidad práctica de protegerse contra los elementos, los zapatos incorporaron rápidamente componentes decorativos más elaborados, así como formas individualizadas. La gran variedad de calzados y maneras de construirlos ha evolucionado de forma vertiginosa en el transcurso de la historia y en el seno de multitud de diferentes culturas.

Actualmente, el calzado y los accesorios constituyen uno de los componentes más imperativos y lucrativos en la industria de la moda. Los diseñadores prestan mayor atención que nunca a los accesorios y, la confianza de los consumidores ha aumentado a un ritmo constante gracias a una mayor oferta de productos deseables. Los accesorios nos brindan una puerta de entrada a la visión del diseñador y cautivan tanto a mujeres como a hombres. Hoy en día, hay revistas, ferias de muestras, grupos de análisis de tendencias, blogs, libros, fetichistas y cursos dedicados exclusivamente al calzado.

El diseño del calzado acaba de experimentar un renacimiento como disciplina creativa. Las nuevas ideas traspasan los límites conocidos y alcanzan nuevos estadios de creatividad. Basta pensar en los últimos desfiles de pasarela para comprender porqué algunos de estos looks extremos reciben la mayor cobertura mediática: los zapatos vuelven a ser el centro de atención.

Este libro pretende dar a conocer a diseñadores que conservan una identidad única e independiente del factor comercial y que además, poseen una fuerte voz propia - tendencias actuales aparte. No todos son únicamente diseñadores de zapatos, pero es tan importante incluir la perspectiva de aquellos que no provienen de la industria del calzado, como la de los diseñadores que trabajan en el sector desde hace años. Hemos incluido a diseñadores de diferentes procedencias geográficas y culturales y que, sin embargo, comparten un único interés: la pasión por los zapatos.

Intitulé Shoe Design, le présent livre a pour objet d'illustrer la richesse de créativité propre au design de chaussures de nos jours. Il y sera question de dessinateurs qui perpétuent la tradition des modèles élégants et plutôt classiques, mais aussi de ceux qui se réclament de l'expérimental et changent ainsi de fond en comble la façon dont nous percevons les chaussures. Les produits taillés sur mesure et d'une individualité rare y trouveront leur place au même titre que les concepts aux allures futuristes – la création de chaussures a tout pour plaire et fasciner tout en préservant la notion de désirabilité.

Tout au long de l'histoire, les chaussures ont joué un rôle essentiel dans l'habillement. Destinées initialement à protéger les pieds contre les éléments, les chaussures vantèrent rapidement une décoration et prirent des formes individuelles. La variété de chaussures et de modèles a fait l'objet d'un développement considérable au cours de l'histoire et à travers les différentes civilisations.

Aujourd'hui, les chaussures et leurs accessoires constituent l'un des secteurs les plus lucratifs et importants de l'industrie de la mode actuelle. Les dessinateurs sont plus attentifs que jamais aux accessoires et la confiance du client est proportionnelle à l'augmentation de la variété des produits désirables disponibles. En outre, les accessoires permettent d'accéder facilement à la vision d'un dessinateur et exercent aussi bien sur les femmes que sur les hommes une fascination envoûtante. A tel point qu'il existe aujourd'hui des magazines et des foires spécialisés, des analyses de tendances, des blogs des livres, des fétichistes et des cours entièrement consacrés aux chaussures.

Secteur inventif, la création de chaussures vient de connaître une renaissance. De nouvelles idées apparaissent, des limites se déplacent, de nouveaux niveaux de créativité sont atteints. Pour comprendre pourquoi quelques-uns parmi ces looks extrêmes font la une des journaux, il suffit de jeter un coup d'œil sur les derniers défilés de mode. Incontestablement, les chaussures sont de retour sur le devant de la scène.

Dans ce livre, nous entendons vous présenter des dessinateurs avec leur identité et leur vocation au-delà de tout raisonnement commercial et tendances en vogue. S'ils ne sont pas forcément tous dessinateurs de chaussures stricto sensu, ils ont certainement leur mot à dire. Par conséquent, il nous a semblé bon de se pencher autant sur ceux qui ne sont pas issus du domaine de la chaussure que sur ceux qui y travaillent depuis des années. Nous avons donc réuni des dessinateurs aux contextes culturels et géographiques divers. Ils partagent tous la même passion : celle des chaussures.

In Shoe Design desideriamo presentarvi l'infinita varietà di idee creative che oggi si riscontra nel settore del design di scarpe. Dai disegnatori che portano avanti la tradizione dei modelli più classici ed eleganti a quelli che amano esplorare campi nuovi e sperimentali cambiando così la nostra percezione generale di idea di calzatura. Dalle scarpe realizzate su misura ai modelli del tutto unici a quelli scaturiti da idee futuristiche, il design di scarpe può essere accattivante e provocatorio, e mantenere allo stesso tempo quel senso di desiderabilità.

Le calzature rappresentano da sempre una parte essenziale del nostro guardaroba. Inizialmente nacquero come risposta al bisogno pratico di proteggersi dagli agenti atmosferici, ma ben presto assunsero decorazioni e forme particolari. I vari tipi di scarpe e i modi di confezionarle hanno registrato un notevole sviluppo nel corso della storia e delle diverse culture che si sono avvicendate.

Calzature e accessori costituiscono una delle nicchie più importanti e redditizie dell'odierna industria della moda. L'attenzione che i designer riservano agli accessori non è mai stata così alta come ora, e la fiducia accordata dai consumatori, che oggi possono scegliere tra un più vasto assortimento di articoli accattivanti, è in continua crescita. Gli accessori offrono una facile via d'accesso nella mente del disegnatore e affascinano tanto le donne quanto gli uomini. Oggi esistono riviste, presentazioni commerciali, specialisti di analisi delle tendenze, blog, libri, fanatici della moda e corsi, tutti dedicati interamente alle calzature.

Negli ultimi anni il design di scarpe ha conosciuto un nuovo periodo di fioritura grazie alla creatività che oggi si riscontra in questo settore, dove stanno emergendo nuove idee avanguardiste che toccano livelli di inventiva mai raggiunti prima. Basti pensare alle ultime sfilate di moda per capire il vero motivo di tanto interesse della stampa per alcuni dei look più estremi: le scarpe.

In questo libro desideriamo presentarvi designer che esprimono la loro personalità del tutto unica senza farsi influenzare dalla commercialità del prodotto, artisti che fanno sentire la propria voce al di là delle mode del momento. Non sono tutti disegnatori di calzature in senso stretto, ma riteniamo che sia importante dare spazio tanto alle idee di coloro che non provengono direttamente da questo settore, quanto a quelle di chi di questo campo è ormai un esperto. Vi sono inclusi disegnatori di tutto il mondo, di diversa origine geografica e culturale, ma con un interesse in comune: la passione per le scarpe.

BORA AKSU | LONDON, UK

www.boraaksu.com

Photos © James Frid, courtesy Bora Aksu (portrait)

1 Converse Customized Patchwork Boots, AW 2004-2005
2 Knit and Leather Boots, AW 2006-2007
3 Hand Knitted Boot Sandals, SS 2006
4 Leather and Knitted Boots, AW 2004-2005
5 Knit and Sheepskin Mixed Leather Boots, AW 2007

Bora Aksu is a Turkish born designer and a Central Saint Martins fashion graduate. As a fashion designer he has always paid the utmost attention to the importance of footwear in his catwalk collections. He has never followed trends and always kept his own vision and integrity. A philosophy that clearly shows in his footwear collections.

Der in der Türkei geborene Designer Bora Aksu absolvierte sein Studium an der Central Saint Martins Hochschule für Kunst und Design. Als Modedesigner standen bei seinen Laufstegkollektionen immer die Schuhe im Mittelpunkt. Nie folgte er Trends, sondern hielt stets an seiner eigenen Vorstellung und Integrität fest. Eine Philosophie, die sich ganz deutlich in seinen Schuhkollektionen widerspiegelt.

Bora Aksu es un diseñador de raíces turcas con un diploma en moda por el instituto de arte y diseño Central Saint Martins. Como diseñador de moda siempre ha otorgado extrema importancia al calzado en sus colecciones para pasarela. Aksu nunca se ha adherido a otras corrientes o tendencias, sino que ha sabido conservar su visión personal y su integridad a lo largo del tiempo. Una filosofía que se manifiesta claramente en sus colecciones.

Né en Turquie, le dessinateur Bora Aksu obtint son diplôme en stylisme au Central Saint Martins. Styliste de mode, Aksu a toujours attaché beaucoup d'importance aux chaussures dans ses collections de défilés. Il n'a jamais suivi les tendances en vogue et a toujours su garder sa vision et son intégrité. Philosophie qui se reflète clairement dans ses collections de chaussures.

Nato in Turchia, il designer Bora Aksu ha compiuto i suoi studi universitari presso il Central Saint Martins College of Art and Design. Anche in veste di stilista di moda, ha sempre conferito alle scarpe il ruolo di protagonista principale delle sue sfilate. Aksu non ha mai seguito le tendenze, scegliendo piuttosto di conservare la sua visione personale e la sua integrità. Una filosofia che si manifesta chiaramente nelle sue collezioni.

4

5

JOSEPH AZAGURY | LONDON, UK

www.josephazagury.com

Photos © Joseph Azagury

1 CP139,Argenro nappa base with Swarovski crystal
   detail, SS 2008
2 CP163, Natural cork, SS 2008
3 CP154, Patent leather with transparent vinyl insert,
   SS 2008
4 CP156, Crepe satin with metallic leather detail, SS 2008

Azagury set up his label in 1990 after studying at Cordwainer's in London and working in Spain, Italy and the US. Each design is carefully drawn and sculpted in London before being crafted in Italy from the highest quality materials. Azagury's styles are elegant, feminine and luxurious.

Azagury studierte am Cordwainers College in London und arbeitete in Spanien, Italien und den USA, bevor er 1990 sein eigenes Label gründete. Jeder seiner Entwürfe wird in London sorgfältig gezeichnet und geformt und danach in Italien aus den qualitativ hochwertigsten Materialien gefertigt. Azagurys Modelle sind elegant, feminin und luxuriös.

Azagury fundó su marca en 1990, después de concluir sus estudios en el instituto Cordwainers de Londres y de ganar experiencia en España, Italia y EE.UU. Cada uno de sus diseños es dibujado y modelado cuidadosamente en Londres antes de ser confeccionado en Italia, usando únicamente materiales de la más alta calidad. Su estilo es elegante, femenino y lujoso.

Azagury fit ses études au Cordwainers à Londres, travailla en Espagne, en Italie et aux Etats-Unis avant de lancer son propre label en 1990. Chacun de ses modèles est soigneusement dessiné et sculpté à Londres, puis fabriqué en Italie à partir de matériaux de la plus haute qualité. Les modèles signés Azagury sont élégants, féminins et luxueux.

Azagury fondò il suo marchio nel 1990 dopo aver studiato presso il Cordwainers College di Londra e aver lavorato in Spagna, in Italia e negli Stati Uniti. Ogni suo modello viene accuratamente disegnato e plasmato a Londra e successivamente confezionato in Italia con l'impiego di materiali di altissima qualità. Lo stile di Azagurys è elegante, femminile e raffinato.

1

2

3

4

GIANNI BARBATO | CIVITANOVA MARCHE, ITALY

www.giannibarbato.it

Photos © Roberto Mazzola - Studio Sancassani-Wanna Granatelli, Wanna Granatelli (portrait)

1 Man's and Woman's boot with metal rivets (hand made), SS 2004
2 Men's shoe in printed crocodile effect gloss, AW 2007 / 08
3 Women's boot with oxidized gold varnish, AW 2004 / 05
4 Transparent python men's boot, SS 2004
5 Men's boot, waxed embroidery on leather with colourful detail, SS 2006
6 Men's laced boot in oxidised and aged skin, AW 2005 / 06
7 Limited edition Cobra boot, June 2004
8 Men's boot, waxed embroidery on leather with colourful detail, SS 2006
9 Special design with metallic mesh, AW 2004 / 05
10 Inlaid heel with semi-precious Cabouchon stones, AW 2005 / 06

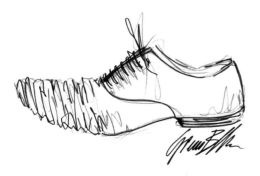

Designing his first shoe collection in 1984, Gianni Barbato has consistently pushed the boundaries of footwear design. He incorporates a wide range of often unexpected and original material mixes and hardware finishes, always with a minute attention to detail. Barbato creates strong silhouettes for women retaining a feminine edge whilst his masculine styles are robust, hardy and unafraid of detail.

1984 entwarf Gianni Barbato seine erste Schuhkollektion. Seitdem hat er die Grenzen des Schuhdesigns immer weiter verschoben. Er arbeitet mit einer Vielzahl von oft unerwarteten und originellen Materialkombinationen und -veredelungen, stets mit großer Liebe zum Detail. Barbato kreiert Damenschuhe mit starken Silhouetten, aber femininem Touch; seine Herrenschuhe sind robust, unempfindlich und beweisen Mut zum Detail.

En 1984 diseñó su primera colección de zapatos y, desde entonces, Gianni Barbato ha empujado sistemáticamente los límites del diseño de calzado. Barbato hace uso de una amplia gama de mezclas de materiales y rotundos acabados a menudo inesperados y originales, siempre prestando la máxima atención a cada detalle. Este diseñador crea marcadas siluetas para mujeres, siempre manteniendo un aire de feminidad. Sus modelos para hombres son robustos, resistentes y tampoco prescinden de los detalles.

Gianni Barbato conçut sa première collection de chaussures en 1984. Depuis, il a constamment repoussé les limites du design de chaussures. Il mise sur une gamme étendue de matériaux mélangés et de finitions souvent inattendues et originelles en attachant une grande importance aux détails. Barbato crée pour les femmes des silhouettes fortes sans omettre la touche de féminité; ses modèles pour homme sont robustes, vigoureux et ne craignent pas le détail.

Gianni Barbato disegnò la sua prima collezione di scarpe nel 1984: da allora il suo nome è sempre stato sinonimo di design all'avanguardia nel settore delle calzature. Le sue creazioni sono frutto della combinazione di una vasta gamma di materiali e rifiniture spesso inaspettati e originali, cui si affianca immancabilmente un'estrema attenzione per il dettaglio. Barbato crea scarpe per donna con silhouette vigorose ma contemporaneamente femminili, mentre i suoi modelli maschili sono robusti, resistenti e senza paura di eccedere nel dettaglio.

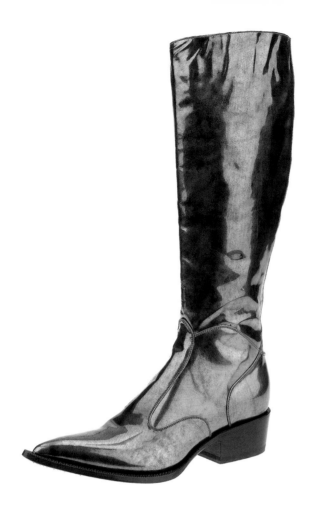

3

4

5

6

9

MANOLO BLAHNIK | LONDON, UK

www.manoloblahnik.com

Photos © Manolo Blahnik, Michael Roberts (portrait)

1 Futtuta, patent leather, Satin, AW 2008 / 09
2 Ebru, leather, SS 2008
3 Bogazici, Marimekko Unikko print with leather
4 Spart, Satin, Leather, AW 2008 / 09
5 Afna, Suede, leather, AW 2008 / 09
6 Knock, Leather, SS 2008
7 Zeynel, Cotton Marimekko print, SS 2008
8 Satine for Christopher Kane, Satin, Leather,
   AW 2008 / 09

Originally from the Canary Islands, Blahnik's designs are sexy, frivolous and feminine. Having always had a huge following, his shoes reached almost magical status after the success of the "Sex and the City" television show, elevating him to one of the most important footwear designers in the world.

Manolo Blahnik wurde auf den kanarischen Inseln geboren. Sein Design ist sexy, frivol und feminin. Er hatte zwar schon immer eine große Fangemeinde, mit dem Erfolg der Fernsehserie „Sex and the City" aber erreichten seine Schuhe Kultstatus und Blahnik selbst avancierte zu einem der wichtigsten Schuhdesigner der Welt.

Manolo Blahnik es originario de las Islas Canarias. Sus diseños son sexy, frívolos y femeninos. Sus creaciones han contado desde siempre con multitud de admiradores y, después del gran éxito de la serie „Sexo en Nueva York", sus zapatos han cobrado un estatus casi mágico, convirtiéndole en uno de los diseñadores de calzado más prestigiosos del mundo.

Manolo Blahnik, originaire des Iles Canaries, conçoit des dessins sexy, frivoles et féminins. Très prisées depuis quelque temps déjà, ces chaussures firent un véritable tabac suite au succès de la série télévisée « Sex and the City » et lui permirent de devenir l'un des plus importants dessinateurs de la planète.

Originario delle Canarie, Blahnik confeziona modelli sexy, frivoli e femminili. Pur avendo sempre raccolto ampi consensi, con il successo della serie televisiva "Sex and the City" le sue scarpe divennero quasi uno status symbol, promuovendo Blahnik a uno dei più importanti disegnatori di scarpe del mondo.

2

3

6

7

8

BRUNO BORDESE | MILAN, ITALY

www.brunobordese.com

Photos © Bruno Bordese

1   Scafo 8561, Crocodile printed Calf, Dark Brown & Scafo
    8562, Crocodile printed Calf, Black, Men's AW 08 / 09
2   Tred 6603, Washed Leather, Natural, Men's SS 2006
3   Loira 6013, Washed Leather, Natural, Women's SS 2006
4   Nova 8852 & Nova 8854, Brown Calf, Women's AW
    08 / 09
5   Muta 8041, Washed Silver Calf, Women's SS 2008
6   Trapezio 8237, Silver Calf, Men's SS 2008

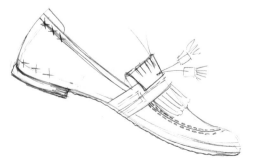

Turin born designer Bruno Bordese has worked with designers such as Vivienne Westwood and Yoji Yamamoto. He launched his Clone brand in 1994, which quickly became a leading Italian directional brand and then followed with the more classically designed, Bruno Bordese brand in 1996. Bordese's designs combine non-conformist ideas with classical Italian heritage resulting in two interesting brands that have made Bordese a leader of contemporary Italian footwear.

Der in Turin geborene Bruno Bordese hat mit Designern wie Vivienne Westwood und Yoji Yamamoto zusammengearbeitet. 1994 brachte er seine Marke Clone heraus, die in Italien schnell zu einem Marktführer wurde; 1996 folgte das eher klassisch ausgerichtete Label Bruno Bordese. Bordeses Design vereint ungewöhnliche Ideen mit klassischen Elementen aus dem italienischen Erbe. Das Ergebnis sind zwei interessante Marken, die Bordese in der italienischen Schuhbranche von heute eine Spitzenposition eingebracht haben.

Nacido en Turín, Bruno Bordese ha trabajado con diseñadores como Vivienne Westwood y Yoji Yamamoto. En 1994 lanzó su marca Clone, que rápidamente se convirtió en un punto de referencia dentro del mercado italiano. Poco después, en 1996, introdujo también la marca Bruno Bordese, que ofrece diseños más clásicos. Sus trabajos combinan ideas de carácter inconformista con el clásico legado italiano. El resultado son dos interesantes marcas que han hecho de Bordese una figura clave en la industria actual del calzado italiano.

Bruno Bordese, designer turinois, a collaboré avec des dessinateurs tels que Vivienne Westwood et Yoji Yamamoto. En 1994, il lança sa marque Clone qui devint rapidement l'un des leaders en Italie; s'ensuivit en 1996 le label Bruno Bordese à vocation plutôt classique. Ses designs mêlent des idées insolites à l'héritage italien classique. Il en résulte deux marques intéressantes qui ont fait de Bordese l'un des tout premiers de la chaussure transalpine d'aujourd'hui.

Nato a Torino, Bruno Bordese ha lavorato con stilisti del calibro di Vivienne Westwood e Yoji Yamamoto. Nel 1994 lanciò la sua marca Clone, che nel mercato italiano è diventata presto un importante punto di riferimento. Il 1996 è stato l'anno della marca più classica Bruno Bordese. I suoi lavori uniscono idee anticonformiste con classiche influenze italiane; il risultato sono due marche interessanti che hanno fatto di Bordese una figura chiave nel mondo attuale delle calzature italiane.

1

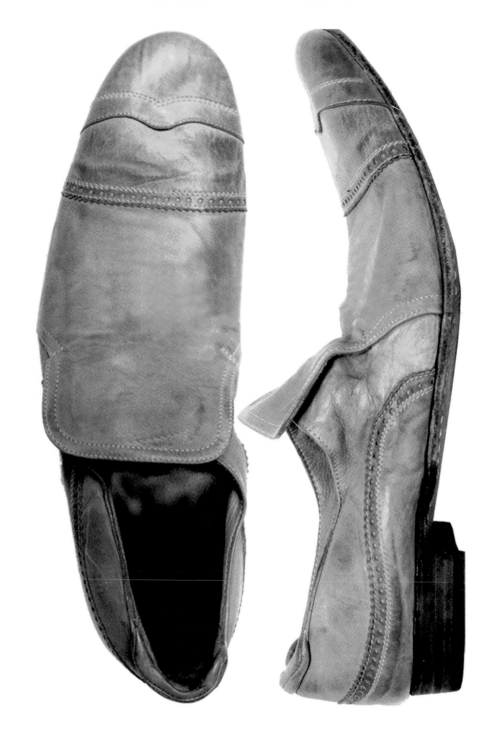

2

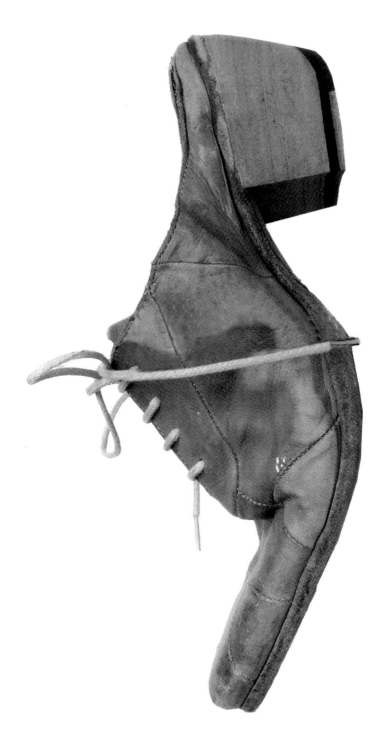

3

4

5

NICOLE BRUNDAGE | HOUSTON (TX), USA

www.nicolebrundage.com

Photos © Jovanka Savic, Sean Beolchini (2)

1 Andi, black suede and black patent, AW 2008 / 09
2 Pippi, Nappa leather, SS 2008
3 Viv, matte calf leather, AW 2008 / 09
4 Tani, matte calf leather with suede, AW 2008 / 09
5 Pippi, Nappa leather, SS 2008

Born in San Antonio, Texas, Nicole Brundage studied Art History before becoming a shoe designer, soon collaborating with Manolo Blahnik to create Zac Posen's autumn / winter 2004 and presenting her first collection in Paris in 2006. Brundage's sensual, fluent and ultra-modern style has seen her making collections for Furla's "Talent Hub" and she currently designs a capsule collection for Salvatore Ferragamo.

Nicole Brundage wurde in San Antonio, Texas, geboren und studierte zunächst Kunstgeschichte, bevor sie Schuhdesignerin wurde. Schon bald entwarf sie in Zusammenarbeit mit Manolo Blahnik die Herbst / Winter-Kollektion 2004 für Zac Posen. Es folgte ihre Debütkollektion 2006 in Paris. Ihr sinnlicher, fließender und ultramoderner Stil brachte ihr eine Teilnahme am Projekt „Talent Hub" des Labels Furla ein. Zurzeit entwirft sie eine Sonderkollektion für Salvatore Ferragamo.

Nicole Brundage nació en San Antonio, Texas y estudió Historia del Arte antes de convertirse en diseñadora de calzado. Brundage trabajó en sus comienzos junto a Manolo Blahnik en la creación de la colección de otoño / invierno 2004 de Zac Posen y, en 2006, presentó su primera colección propia en París. Su estilo sensual, fluido y ultramoderno ha sido plasmado en diseños para el „Talent Hub" de Furla. En la actualidad esta diseñadora trabaja en una colección cápsula para Salvatore Ferragamo.

Née à San Antonio au Texas, Nicole Brundage étudia l'histoire de l'art avant de devenir dessinatrice de chaussures et travailler peu de temps après avec Manolo Blahnik sur la collection automne / hiver 2004 de Zac Posen. En 2006, elle présenta sa première collection à Paris. Son style sensuel, fluide et ultramoderne lui permit de dessiner des collections pour le projet « Talent Hub » de Furla. En attendant la collection spéciale pour Salvatore Ferragamo.

Nata a San Antonio, in Texas, Nicole Brundage studiò storia dell'arte prima di diventare una stilista di scarpe. Dopo breve tempo, in collaborazione con Manolo Blahnik, firmò la collezione autunno / inverno 2004 per Zac Posen, per poi debuttare a Parigi nel 2006. Il suo stile sensuale, fluente e ultramoderno le ha procurato l'incarico di realizzare alcuni modelli per il marchio "Talent Hub" di Furla; attualmente è impegnata nella creazione di una capsule collection per Salvatore Ferravamo.

1

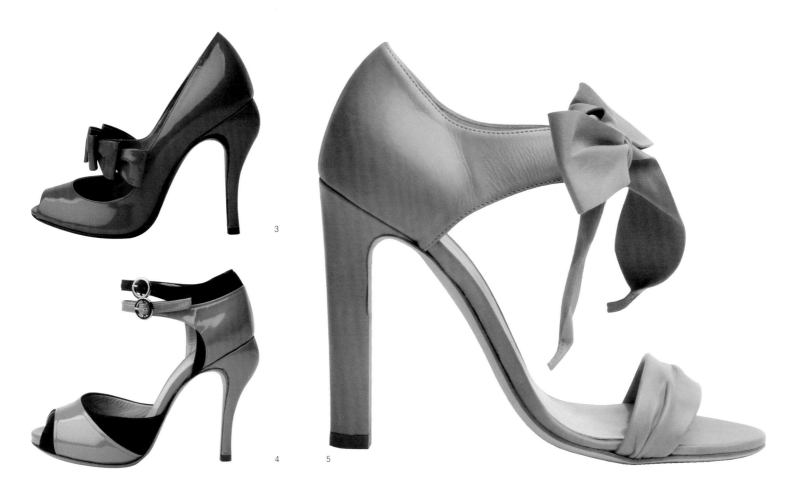

3

4

5

CARRÉDUCKER | LONDON, UK
Deborah Carré & James Ducker

www.carreducker.com

Photos © Keith Leighton (1), Guy Hills (2, 4, 7), carréducker
(3, 6), Jerry Mason (5), Patrick Boyd (8), Andrew Shields
(portrait)

1   Chisel shoe charm with brilliant diamond stud on black
    box calf oxford shoe
2   Dashing tweed "Winkers" slipper in Yellow Raver,
    prototype A / W 2007
3   Scarlet lined, bespoke derby in box calf with lizard
    detail, 2007
4   Bespoke "boxer" boots in Dashing Tweed with oxblood
    lizard detail, 2007
5   Low-rise saddle boot, made-to-order collection, 2005
6   Bespoke patent dance shoe with white patent
    "go-faster" stripes, 2007
7   Equus thigh boots (press sample)
8   Equus knee boots (press sample)

Injecting a touch of glamour into the traditional world of bespoke shoemaking, Deborah Carré and James Ducker met whilst apprenticing with a master shoemaker for John Lobb. Working closely with their customers, carréducker's shoes are far from staid using modern details, finest quality leathers and innovative materials such as beautifully blended tweed incorporating woven reflective threads to give their designs a contemporary edge.

Deborah Carré und James Ducker bringen eine Portion Glanz in die traditionelle Welt der Maßschuhanfertigung. Die beiden lernten sich während ihrer Ausbildung beim Meister-Schuhmacher John Lobb kennen. Sie legen Wert auf eine enge Zusammenarbeit mit ihren Kunden. Carréducker-Schuhe sind alles andere als bieder: Durch moderne Details, feinste Qualitätsleder und originelle Materialien, wie Tweedmischungen mit gewebten, reflektierenden Fäden, erhalten ihre Designs einen zeitgemäßen Touch.

Deborah Carré y James Ducker se conocieron cuando trabajaban de aprendices para un maestro zapatero de la firma John Lobb. Hoy añaden un toque de glamour al tradicional mundo del diseño de calzados a medida y apuestan por una cooperación estrecha con los clientes. Los modelos de Carréducker quedan lejos de ser aburridos gracias la añadidura de detalles modernos, el empleo de cueros de primera calidad y el uso de materiales innovadores como, por ejemplo, los tejidos tweed, que incluyen bordados con hilos reflectantes.

Deborah Carré et James Ducker apportent une touche de glamour au monde traditionnel de la cordonnerie sur mesure. Ils se sont rencontrés lors de leur formation auprès d'un maître cordonnier travaillant pour John Lobb. Ils coopèrent étroitement avec leurs clients et leurs chaussures sont loin d'être ennuyeuses. L'utilisation de détails modernes, de cuirs de la plus haute qualité et de matériaux innovants avec en prime un joli mélange de tweed agrémenté de fils réflecteurs tissés confère à leurs designs un aspect contemporain.

Deborah Carré e James Ducker si sono conosciuti durante il loro periodo di apprendistato per conto di un maestro delle calzature dell'impresa James Lobb. Oggi donano un tocco di glamour al tradizionale mondo delle scarpe su misura e puntano su una stretta collaborazione con i clienti. Le scarpe Carrèducker sono tutt'altro che noiose: grazie ai loro dettagli moderni, all'elevata qualità del cuoio utilizzato e ai materiali innovativi, come tweed meravigliosamente lavorato con fili riflettenti, i modelli di questa linea si distinguono per il loro stile contemporaneo.

2

5

6

7

8

PIERRE CORTHAY | PARIS, FRANCE
Pierre Corthay, Christophe Corthay

www.corthay.fr

Photos © M. Alberto Martinez, Stéphanie Fraisse (portraits)

1 Bucy, green bronze calf, leather sole, internal beveled waist
2 Django, green bronze calf and light tobacco calf, leather sole, square waist
3 Arca, natural python, leather sole with white stitching, internal beveled waist
4 Wild, sidelace crocodile, leather sole, internal and external beveld waist
5 Arca, raspberry patent calf, leather sole, internal beveled waist
6 Arca, orange minium patent calf, leather sole, internal beveled waist
7 Jouvet, old wood calf, leather sole, internal beveled waist
8 Arca, crimson calf, leather sole, internal beveled waist

Corthay gained his years of experience with John Lobb of London and Berluti in Paris, both masters of the men's footwear field. This luxury menswear label offers handmade to measure service alongside its ready-to-wear collections. Featuring interesting lasts and material mixes Corthay has a flagship store in Paris and three shops in Japan.

Corthay sammelte bei John Lobb in London und Berluti in Paris Erfahrungen, beide Meister im Bereich Herrenschuhe. Das Luxuslabel für Herren bietet neben seinen Prêt-à-porter-Kollektionen auch von Hand gefertigte, maßgeschneiderte Modelle an. Corthay verwendet interessante Leisten- und Materialmischungen und hat einen Flagship-Store in Paris sowie drei Läden in Japan.

Corthay ganó experiencia trabajando para John Lobb en Londres y Berluti en París, ambos verdaderos maestros de la moda del calzado masculino. Esta marca de lujo para hombres ofrece piezas hechas a medida, así como colecciones prêt-à-porter. Trabaja con mezclas de hormas y materiales muy interesantes, y sus creaciones están a la venta en su boutique principal de París y sus tres filiales en Japón.

Corthay acquit son savoir-faire chez John Lobb à Londres et Berluti à Paris, tous deux maîtres de la chaussure pour homme. Outre ses collections prêt-à-porter, son label de luxe pour hommes propose également des modèles faits sur mesure. Corthay utilise des mélanges intéressants d'embauchoirs et de matériaux. Il compte une boutique vitrine à Paris et trois magasins au Japon.

Corthay è cresciuto professionalmente al fianco di John Lobb a Londra e Berluti a Parigi, entrambi maestri nel campo delle calzature per uomo. Oltre a collezioni prêt-à-porter, questo prestigioso marchio di scarpe maschili comprende modelli confezionati a mano e articoli realizzati su misura. Corthay utilizza un interessante miscuglio di forme e materiali; la sede principale della sua griffe è a Parigi, ma si contano tre negozi anche in Giappone.

8

ERNESTO ESPOSITO | NAPLES, ITALY

www.ernestoespositoshoes.com

Photos © Confashionstudio, Ernesto Esposito (portrait)

1 BOOTIE, Soft nappa leather bootie with chain and metal skulls, stars, SS 2003
2 Double platform with ticker (chunky) heel and t-strap in mix of metallic python and leather
3 Ankle strap metal sandals with platform and stripes of leather covering heel and platform
4 Double platform and squared heel in multi stripe metallic leather
5 Sling back with metallic leather covered in net
6 Middle heel with t-strap sandals in metal leather with interior platform
7 Victor-Victoria,Black patent derby with inner platform and metal piping
8 Pietra nascosta, Pump with Swarowsky „hidden stone" wrapt in a bow with inner platform
9 Butterfly, Sling back with metal peach silk leather combined with black suede butterfly
10 Vamp, Double bow suede platform with french dentelle

Besides working on his own brand, Esposito has worked with some of the most prestigious fashion brands in the world from Marc Jacobs and Sergio Rossi to Chloé and Louis Vuitton. His main source of inspiration and personal passion is contemporary art, which shows in his modern and forward thinking designs.

Neben der Arbeit an seinem eigenen Label hat Esposito bereits für einige der angesehensten Modemarken der Welt gearbeitet: von Marc Jacobs und Sergio Rossi über Chloé bis hin zu Louis Vuitton. Seine Hauptinspirationsquelle und persönliche Leidenschaft ist die zeitgenössische Kunst, die sich in seinen modernen und innovativen Designs widerspiegelt.

Aparte de en su propia marca, Esposito ha trabajado con algunas de las casas de moda más prestigiosas del mundo, desde Marc Jacobs y Sergio Rossi hasta Chloé y Louis Vuitton. Su principal fuente de inspiración y, al mismo tiempo, pasión personal es el arte contemporáneo, predilección que se refleja claramente en sus diseños modernos e innovadores.

Non content de s'investir pour sa propre marque, Esposito collabora également avec quelques-unes des marques de mode les plus prestigieuses du monde : Marc Jacobs, Sergio Rossi, Chloé, Louis Vuitton. L'art contemporain est sa première source d'inspiration et aussi sa passion ce qui se reflète dans ses designs modernes et progressistes.

Oltre a lavorare per la sua marca, Esposito ha già collaborato con le griffe più prestigiose del mondo: da Marc Jacobs e Sergio Rossi a Chloé fino a Louis Vuitton. La sua principale fonte d'ispirazione e passione personale è l'arte contemporanea, che si riflette nei suoi design moderni e innovativi.

2 3

4 5

7

8

JOHN FLUEVOG | VANCOUVER, CANADA

www.fluevog.com

Photos © Fluevog, Stephen Wilde (portrait)

1   10th Anniversary Body Parts Pump, Fall 2007
2   Mini Pipsqueak, Spring 2008
3   Teapot Ceylon, Spring 2008
4   Blind Faith Hi Nicolette, Spring 2008
5   Executor Luciano, Spring 2007
6   Style and Grace Brando, Fall 2007

Fluevog and his longtime friend and ex-partner, Peter Fox, founded Fox & Fluevog, in 1970, on finding and opening an old warehouse full of vintage, dead-stock footwear. Around 1980, Fox left to start his own brand and Fluevog took over the business designing the new styles and building it into the multinational shoe brand it is today. Design detail and comfort are key to Fluevog's style.

John Fluevog und sein langjähriger Freund und Ex-Partner Peter Fox gründeten Fox & Fluevog 1970. Sie hatten eine alte Lagerhalle voll mit altmodischen und unverkauften Schuhen erworben und eröffneten diese. Um das Jahr 1980 herum stieg Fox aus, um sein eigenes Label zu gründen. Fluevog übernahm das Geschäft, entwarf neue Modelle und machte die Marke zu der internationalen Schuhmarke, die sie heute ist. Detail und Komfort charakterisieren Fluevogs Stil.

Fluevog fundó junto con su amigo de toda la vida y antiguo socio, Peter Fox, la marca Fox & Fluevog cuando, en 1970, encontraron y compraron juntos un viejo almacén lleno de zapatos pasados de moda. Allá por 1980, Fox abandonó la empresa para lanzar su propia marca. Fluevog asumió el mando y creó nuevos diseños, convirtiendo su empresa en la marca multinacional de calzados que es hoy. El estilo de Fluevog se caracteriza por sus detalles y comodidad.

En 1970, John Fluevog fonda Fox & Fluevog avec son ami de longue date et ex-partenaire Peter Fox après avoir trouvé et ouvert un ancien dépôt plein de vieilles chaussures invendues. Vers 1980, Fox s'en alla lancer sa propre marque. Fluevog reprit le label, conçut les nouveaux modèles et hissa la marque de chaussures au niveau internationale qui est le sien aujourd'hui. Détail et confort caractérisent le style de Fluevog.

Nel 1970 John Fluevog e il suo amico di lunga data nonché ex-socio Peter Fox fondarono Fox & Fluevog, acquistando e riaprendo i battenti di un vecchio capannone pieno di vecchie scarpe mai vendute. Intorno al 1980 Fox si staccò dalla società per fondare un suo marchio personale, e Fluevog rilevò l'azienda disegnando nuovi modelli e trasformandola nell'impresa multinazionale che conosciamo oggi. Dettagli di design e comodità sono le principali caratteristiche che definiscono lo stile di Fluevog.

2

3

4

5

6

BRUNO FRISONI | PARIS, FRANCE

www.brunofrisoni.com

Photos © Bruno Frisoni, Matthieu Salvaing (portrait)

1 Patent leather, AW 2008-2009
2 Satin silk, AW 2008-2009
3 Satin Silk, AW 2008-2009
4 Patent leather and elastic band, AW 2008-2009
5 Satin silk and elastic band, AW 2008-2009
6 Patent leather, SS 2008
7 Patent leather and straw, SS 2008

Bruno Frisoni is one of the most important women's shoe designers in the world. His much coveted shoes take the notion of sensuality to another level being not only sexy but also elegant whilst retaining a modern edge. Besides his own label, Frisoni is also the creative director of the legendary Parisian luxury house, Roger Vivier.

Bruno Frisoni zählt weltweit zu den wichtigsten Designern von Damenschuhen. Seine begehrten Schuhe definieren den Begriff Sinnlichkeit neu – sie sind nicht nur sexy, sondern auch elegant, mit einem modernen Akzent. Neben seinem eigenen Label arbeitet Frisoni außerdem noch als Kreativchef für die legendäre Pariser Luxusmarke Roger Vivier.

Bruno Frisoni es uno de los diseñadores de calzado para mujeres más famosos del mundo. Sus codiciados zapatos llevan el concepto de sensualidad a otra dimensión, ya que combinan lo sexy con lo elegante sin prescindir de un aire moderno. Al margen de su propia marca, Frisoni se ocupa de la dirección creativa de la legendaria firma de lujo parisina Roger Vivier.

Bruno Frisoni figure parmi les plus importants dessinateurs de chaussures pour femmes dans le monde. Objets de convoitise, ses chaussures redéfinissent la notion de sensualité en allant au delà de l'aspect sexy pour atteindre une élégance accompagnée d'une touche moderne. Outre son propre label, Frisoni travaille aussi comme directeur créatif de Roger Vivier, la mythique maison de luxe parisienne.

Bruno Frisoni è uno dei designer di scarpe femminili più importanti a livello mondiale. Le sue richiestissime scarpe definiscono un nuovo concetto di sensualità: non sono solamente sexy, ma anche eleganti con un tocco di modernità. Oltre a gestire la sua marca personale, Frisoni è anche il creativo direttore della leggendaria e prestigiosa casa di scarpe parigina Roger Vivier.

2

3

5

6

7

CINDY GLASS | PARIS, FRANCE
Laya Rahman

www.cindyglass.net

Photos © Laya Rahman, Mona Awad (portrait)

1 Smoking, W 2008-2009
2 Beirut, SS 2006
3 London, SS 2006
4 Madrid, SS 2006
5 Rainbow, SS 2008
6 Clarck Bag, W 2008-2009
7 Papillon, W 2008-2009
8 Saxophone, W 2008-2009

Laya Rahman started off her career as a photographer, actress and film maker. Feeling incomplete with the 2D world, she decided to get back into design and spontaneously chose footwear design. Her love of shoes and hours spent with a shoemaker in Beirut, helped her draw out her own personal style. Cindy Glass was started in 2005 and Rahman opened her first Paris shop in 2007 and has plans to design furniture in the future.

Laya Rahman begann ihre Karriere als Fotografin, Schauspielerin und Filmemacherin. Unzufrieden, auf die 2-D-Welt beschränkt zu sein, beschloss sie, sich dem Design zu widmen. Die Wahl fiel spontan auf Schuhdesign. Ihre Liebe zu Schuhen und die Zeit bei einem Schuhmacher in Beirut halfen ihr dabei, ihren eigenen Stil zu entwickeln. Das Label Cindy Glass wurde 2005 gegründet; 2007 eröffnete Rahman ihr erstes Geschäft in Paris. Sie plant, in Zukunft Möbel zu entwerfen.

Laya Rahman inició su carrera como fotógrafa, actriz y cineasta, aunque este mundo bidimensional no consiguió satisfacer del todo sus aspiraciones y la empujó de nuevo al diseño, más concretamente al diseño de calzado. Su pasión por los zapatos, así como las muchas horas que compartió con un zapatero en Beirut, contribuyeron a que desarrollara un estilo personal. La marca Cindy Glass cobró vida en 2005 y, en 2007, Rahman inauguró su primera tienda en París. Sus proyectos futuros pasan por el diseño de muebles.

Laya Rahman lança sa carrière comme photographe, actrice et cinéaste. Ne pouvant s'épanouir dans le 2D, elle se tourna vers le design en optant spontanément pour celui de la chaussure. Sa passion pour les souliers et le temps passé à Beyrouth auprès d'un cordonnier l'ont aidée à se forger son propre style. En 2005, fut lancée la marque Cindy Glass et en 2007, Rahman ouvrit sa première boutique à Paris. A l'avenir, elle envisage de concevoir des meubles.

Laya Rahman iniziò la sua carriera come fotografa, attrice e produttrice cinematografica. Ma il mondo bidimensionale non riuscì a soddisfarla e decise così di dedicarsi al design, dove la sua scelta cadde immediatamente sulle scarpe. Il suo amore per quest'ultime e il tempo passato da un calzolaio a Beirut la aiutarono a sviluppare il suo stile personale. La marca Cindy Glass fu fondata nel 2005, e nel 2007 la Rahman inaugurò il suo primo negozio a Parigi. In futuro l'artista ha intenzione di dedicarsi al settore del design di arredi.

1

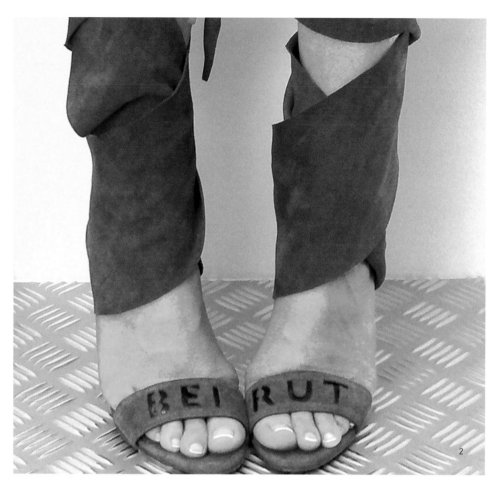

2

3

2

4

6   7

CAROLINE GROVES | LONDON, UK

www.carolinegroves.co.uk

Photos © Joe Lacey (1-6), Michael Tummings (7-9, portrait)

1 Open side peep toe Roso Luce cashemire suede quarters, vintage emerald green croc vamp & heel covers, Jewel red grosgrain binding & original 40's button trim, 2005
2 Zeffarano cashemire suede & turquoise grosgrain slingbacks with platform, Polka dot details & roll trim, 2005
3 Cup back peep toe in Melanzana aniline calf with foxglove pink grosgrain binding & pom pom, 2004
4 Curvaceous but stripey peep toe, high cut vamp in Cucio aniline calf & rost cashemire suede, cerise grosgrain & sculpted toe nose detail, 2007
5 Classic nero cashemire suede "Betty Boop" fully enclosed platform shoe with swirl bow & Argent grey grosgrain binding, 2005
6 Open side closed toe platform shoe, Ultra violet cashemire suede with vintage purple croc heel covers, florence blue grosgrain binding & trinckety trim, 2007
7 Red french calf high platform peep toes with LIPS, 2007
8 Open side peep toe platform shoes in Ultra violet cashemire suede & leather with patchwork detail, Florence blue grosgrain trim & double bow, 2006
9 selection of Caroline's period beechwood lasts

Caroline Groves is a bespoke designer and shoemaker. Groves specialises in exotic and vintage inspired high heeled styles developed through a collaboration with the client resulting in truly unique shoes. Groves has a dedicated following and is currently a member of the London College of Fashion Advisory Board and a freeman of the Worshipful Company of Cordwainers.

Caroline Groves ist eine Designerin und Schuhmacherin, die ihre Arbeiten nach Maß fertigt. Ihr Spezialgebiet sind exotische, vom Vintage-Stil beeinflusste High-Heel-Modelle, die sie in Zusammenarbeit mit ihren Kunden entwickelt. Das Ergebnis sind wahrlich einzigartige Schuhe. Groves hat eine feste Anhängerschaft und ist zurzeit Mitglied des Beratungsausschusses des London College of Fashion.

Caroline Groves diseña y crea zapatos y moda a medida. La diseñadora se ha especializado en el desarrollo de estilos de calzado de tacón exóticos y de inspiración vintage. Cada uno de sus modelos, diseñados en estrecha colaboración con el cliente, es una pieza única. Groves cuenta con muchos seguidores y, en la actualidad, forma parte de la junta consultiva del London College of Fashion y es miembro de honor de la Worshipful Company of Cordwainers, una entidad que se propone fomentar la industria del calzado y promover la formación en este campo.

Dessinatrice et cordonnière, Caroline Groves confectionne sur mesure avec pour spécialisation des modèles à talons hauts exotiques et inspirées du vintage, modèles qu'elle développe en coopération avec ses clients. Cela débouche sur des chaussures tout simplement uniques. Groves peut compter sur une importante communauté de supporters. Actuellement, elle est membre du London College of Fashion Advisory Board et membre d'honneur au Worshipful Company of Cordwainers.

Caroline Groves disegna e crea calzature su misura. La sua specialità sono le scarpe con i tacchi alti di ispirazione esotica e vintage, e ogni suo modello è assolutamente unico in quanto creato in base alle richieste specifiche del cliente. La Groves vanta una solida clientela e attualmente fa parte del comitato di consulenza del College of Fashion di Londra ed è membro onorario della Worshipful Company of Cordwainers.

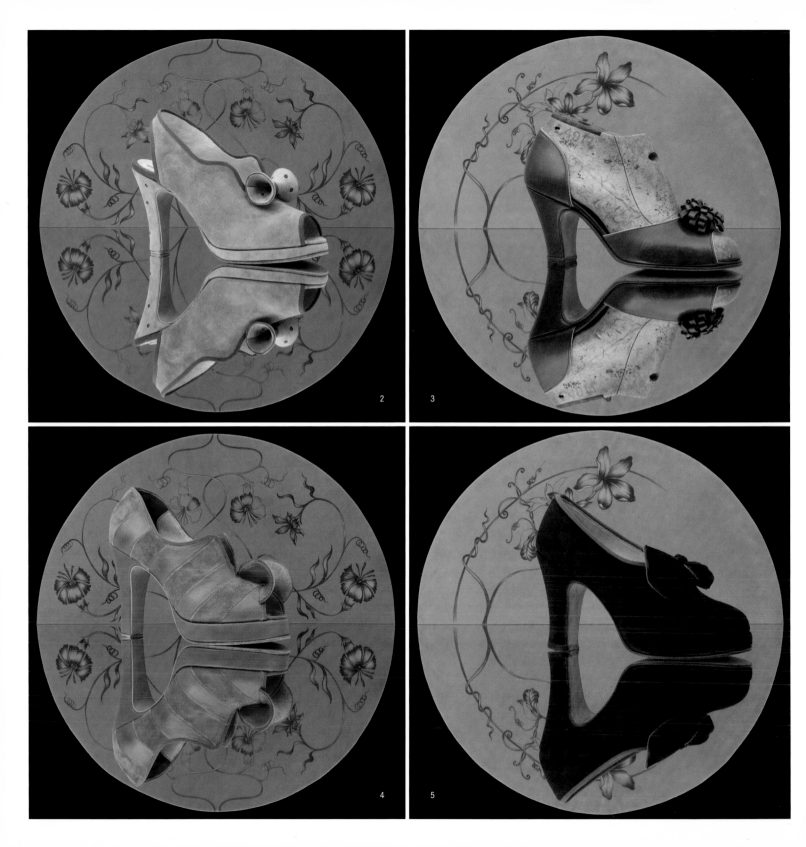

7

8

TERRY DE HAVILLAND | LONDON, UK

www.terrydehavilland.com

Photos © James Frid

1 BOWIE BOOT, created in gold kid leather and laser printed silk, 2005
2 LIZZIE, 70s vintage snakeskins using a combination of gold spotfoil python and gold cobra, 1993
3 SWEETHEART, hand carved, high lacquered wooden wedge with a gold metallic kid suede vamp, 2006
4 ZAP POW, crafted in hand painted canvas, 2007
5 KAIZU, hand carved, high lacquered wooden wedge with a gold python upper, 2006
6 ELECTRA, red kid suede and glazed python, 2003
7 VENUS, gold whipsnake and laser printed silk, 2006
8 MARGAUX, combination of gold whipsnake and gold spotfoil python, 2005

Terry de Havilland is the undisputed king of the platform. He was born into a shoemaking family, starting his footwear career in the 1950's. His designs combine eye-catching colour combinations with decorative detail. After decades in the industry De Havilland continues to design his collections with a huge celebrity following.

Terry de Havilland ist der unumstrittene König der Plateauschuhe. Er wurde in eine Familie von Schuhmachern hineingeboren und startete seine Karriere im Schuhmacherhandwerk in den 1950er-Jahren. Seine Designs vereinen auffallende Farbkombinationen und dekorative Details. Nach Jahrzehnten in der Industrie entwirft de Havilland weiterhin Kollektionen, die sich bei vielen Prominenten großer Beliebtheit erfreuen.

Terry de Havilland es el rey indiscutible de los zapatos de plataforma. Nació en el seno de una familia de fabricantes de calzado e inició su propia carrera en los años 50. Sus diseños combinan los colores llamativos con detalles ornamentales. Después de trabajar durante décadas en la industria zapatera, De Havilland continúa diseñando sus colecciones y posee un sinfín de admiradores célebres.

Terry de Havilland est le roi incontesté de la chaussure à plateaux. Issue d'une famille de cordonniers, il entama sa carrière dans la chaussure dans les années 50. Ses designs rassemblent des combinaisons de couleurs voyantes et des détails décoratifs. Dans l'industrie depuis des décennies, de Havilland conçoit toujours ses collections pour le plus grand bonheur de ses célèbres admirateurs.

Terry de Havilland è il re indiscusso della scarpa con la zeppa. Nacque da una famiglia di produttori artigianali di scarpe e avviò la sua carriera in questo campo intorno al 1950. I suoi modelli combinano colori sgargianti con dettagli decorativi. Impegnato da vari decenni in questo settore, De Havilland continua tuttora a disegnare collezioni che raccolgono numerosi consensi tra le celebrità.

2

3

7

HEDERUS FOR K-SWISS | LONDON, UK
Julia Hederus

www.hederusforkswiss.com

Photos © K-Swiss

1 Blocks, white calf-leather, 2008
2 High Blocks in design progress
3 High Blocks, white calf-leather, 2008
4 Cubes, white calf-leather, 2008
5 High Blocks, Cubes, Blocks, white calf-leather, 2008

In 2006, Julia Hederus approached K-Swiss to develop a collection of innovative sneakers to complement her MA menswear collection for Central St. Martin's. Her interpretation of the classic K-Swiss shoe has lead to K-Swiss producing three of her designs in a limited run of 500 pairs per style to be distributed worldwide. The designs are playful and clean with a futuristic edge bought on by the iconic block shapes that Julia Hederus has become synonymous for.

Julia Hederus wandte sich 2006 an K-Swiss mit der Bitte, im Rahmen ihres Masterstudienganges am Central Saint Martin's eine Kollektion origineller Sneakers entwerfen zu können, um ihre Herrenkollektion zu vervollständigen. Ihre Interpretation des klassischen K-Swiss-Schuhs veranlasste K-Swiss dazu, drei ihrer Entwürfe in einer limitierten Auflage von 500 Paaren pro Modell zu produzieren und diese weltweit zu vermarkten. Die Designs sind verspielt und klar mit einem futuristischen Touch dank der kultigen Blockformen, die zu Hederus Markenzeichen geworden sind.

En 2006, la estudiante del instituto Central Saint Martins, Julia Hederus, se dirigió a K-Swiss para proponer el desarrollo de una colección innovadora de zapatillas en el marco de sus estudios de moda masculina. Su interpretación del clásico zapato K-Swiss fue acogida con gran interés y se produjeron tres de sus diseños para su distribución a nivel mundial en una edición limitada de 500 piezas por modelo. Sus diseños son divertidos y limpios, y poseen un toque futurista gracias a las icónicas formas de bloque que se han convertido ya en marca de su estilo.

En 2006, Julia Hederus se renseigna auprès de K-Swiss pour développer une collection de sneakers originales afin de compléter sa collection pour hommes dans le cadre de son master au Central Saint Martins. Son interprétation de la chaussure classique K-Swiss plut tellement au label que celui-ci décida de fabriquer trois de ses designs dans un tirage limité de 500 paires par modèle afin de les distribuer dans le monde entier. Les designs sont enjoués et clairs avec une touche futuriste en raison des blocs qui sont devenus la forme iconique phare de Julia Hederus.

Nel 2006 Julia Hederus si è rivolta a K-Swiss per realizzare una collezione di scarpe da ginnastica innovative a conclusione del suo corso di studi presso il Central Saint Martin College of Art. La sua interpretazione dei classici modelli K-Swiss ha convinto quest'ultima a mettere in produzione tre delle sue creazioni in un numero limitato di 500 paia per modello da distribuire su scala mondiale. Il design è giocoso e pulito, con una vena futuristica suggerita dalle tipiche forme geometriche per le quali la Hederus è diventata famosa.

1

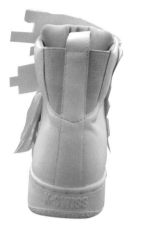

2   3

2   4

5

JAN JANSEN | AMSTERDAM, THE NETHERLANDS

www.janjansenshoes.com

Photos © Joost Guntenaar, Claude Vanheye,
Lok Jansen (portrait)

1 Steely Snake, Calf, Python, Stainless steel, 1993
2 Kiss me on the couch, Suede, Innersole and heel cover
  in 1 piece, 1979
3 Kissing the Pope's toe, Metallic goat, Metallic sprayed
  floating wedge, 1990
4 Woody, Calf nailed on wooden sole, 1969
5 Fong Leng, Suede applied with metallic silver kid flames,
  1974

Dutch designer Jan Jansen has run his label since 1964. His early footwear explorations from the past decades include "floating" wedges, the bamboo shoe, and fashion clogs. Still working from his Amsterdam base, he continues to create designs full of innovation and interesting material mixes. To mark his 45th year as a designer, he recently auctioned off some of his collection at Christie's in London.

Das Label des niederländischen Designers Jan Jansen gibt es seit 1964. In seinen Schuhkollektionen der letzten Jahrzehnte finden sich „schwebende" Keilabsätze, der Bambusschuh und modische Clogs. Jansen arbeitet noch immer von Amsterdam aus und entwirft weiterhin Designs voller Innovation und interessanter Materialmischungen. Um sein 45-jähriges Jubiläum als Designer gebührend zu begehen, hat er vor kurzem einen Teil seiner Kollektion im Auktionshaus Christie's in London versteigert.

Desde 1964, el diseñador neerlandés Jan Jansen dirige su propia marca. Sus tempranas incursiones en el mundo del calzado durante las últimas décadas incluyen los tacones "flotantes", el zapato de bambú y los zuecos a la moda. Todavía con base en Ámsterdam, Jansen sigue creando desde allí diseños muy innovadores elaborados con interesantes mezclas de materiales. Para celebrar su 45 aniversario como diseñador subastó hace poco algunas piezas de su colección en la casa de subastas Christie's en Londres.

Le dessinateur néerlandais Jan Jansen gère son label depuis 1964. Ses premières collections des décennies passées regroupent des talons compensés « flottants », la chaussure bambou et des sabots modernes. Il travaille toujours depuis Amsterdam où il continue à créer des designs pleins d'inventivité et d'intéressants mariages de matériaux. Pour fêter dignement son 45ème anniversaire en tant que dessinateur, il a récemment vendu aux enchères une partie de sa collection chez Christie's à Londres.

La marca del designer neerlandese Jan Jansen esiste dal 1964. Tra le sue prime collezioni, venute alla luce nell'arco degli ultimi decenni, spiccano zeppe "fluttuanti", la scarpa di bambù e zoccoli alla moda. Oggi Jansen lavora ancora ad Amsterdam, dove continua a creare modelli innovativi realizzati con un interessante assortimento di materiali. Per festeggiare in il suo 45° anniversario di attività, di recente Jansen ha messo all'asta una parte della sua collezione nella sala d'aste Christie's di Londra.

2

3

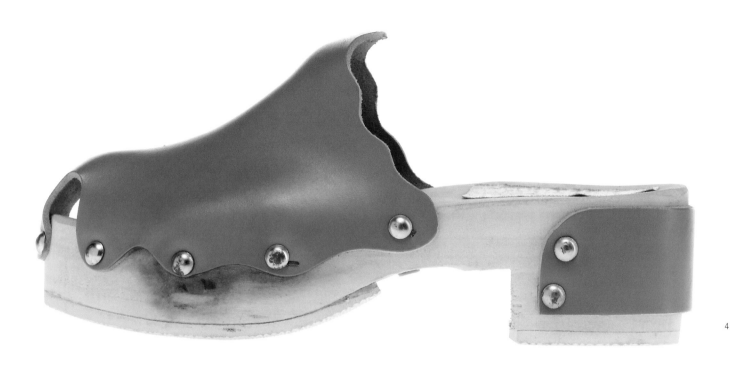

4

KEI KAGAMI | LONDON, UK

www.keikagami.com

Photos © Tessa Oksanen, Courtesy of Kei Kagami (3–6, portrait)

1 yellow-brown cracked leather shoes with adjustable screw heel made of brass, AW 2006 / 07
2 black leather shoe with rusty metal heel as a candle stand, AW 2003 / 04
3 series of shoes from a collection titled, neo-gothic, with molded soles by vegetable leather and oxidized metal heels, AW 2007 / 08
4 white and brown leather shoe expressing fetishism between man and woman, SS 2005

Japanese born Kei Kagami studied architecture and tailoring in Japan, and soon afterwards ended up working for John Galliano in London. Upon finishing his MA in Fashion at Central Saint Martins College of Art and Design he decided to launch his eponymous fashion label with a strong emphasis on footwear. His collections are a wonderful mixture of fantasy, volume, architecture and engineering. His work is both moving and lyrical.

Der in Japan geborene Kei Kagami studierte Architektur und Schneiderei in seinem Heimatland und arbeitete danach für John Galliano in London. Nach seinem Master-Abschluss in Mode am Central Saint Martins College of Art and Design entschied sich Kei Kagami, die gleichnamige Modemarke mit dem Schwerpunkt auf Schuhen zu gründen. Seine Kollektionen sind eine wundervolle Mischung aus Fantasie, Volumen, Architektur und Technik. Seine Arbeiten sind zugleich bewegend und lyrisch.

El diseñador de origen japonés Kei Kagami estudió arquitectura y confección en su país natal. Poco después de terminar sus estudios trabajó para John Galliano en Londres. Tras cursar un master en moda por el instituto de arte y diseño Central Saint Martins College, Kagami decidió lanzar su marca de moda epónima, que está principalmente enfocada al calzado. Sus colecciones son una maravillosa mezcla de fantasía, volumen, arquitectura e ingeniería. Sus creaciones son líricas y conmovedoras.

Né au Japon, Kei Kagami fit ses études d'architecture et de couture dans son pays natal, puis travailla pour John Galliano à Londres. Après avoir décroché son master en mode au Central Saint Martins College of Art and Design, il décida de lancer sa marque de mode éponyme avec un accent particulier sur les chaussures. Dans ses collections, il mélange de façon merveilleuse fantaisie, volume, architecture et technique. Ses réalisations sont à la fois touchantes et lyriques.

Nato in Giappone, Kei Kagami studiò architettura e sartoria nel suo Paese d'origine e poco dopo finì a lavorare per John Galliano a Londra. Dopo aver concluso il master in Moda presso il Central Saint Martins College of Art and Design, decise di lanciare la sua omonima griffe focalizzandosi soprattutto sulle calzature. Le sue collezioni sono un meraviglioso connubio di fantasia, volume, architettura e ingegneria. Le sue opere sono allo stesso tempo commoventi e liriche.

1

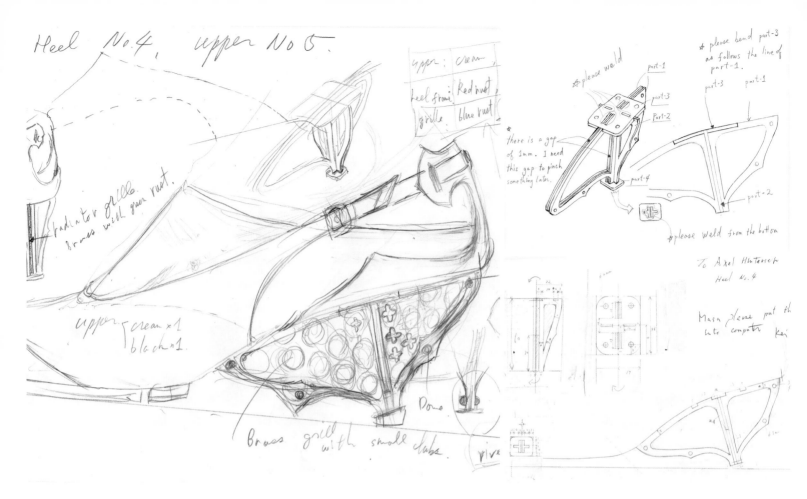

Heel No.4, upper No.5.

upper:	cream
heel frame	Red rust
grille	blue rust

radiator grille.
Brass with green rust.

upper { cream x1
         black x1.

Brass grill with small clubs.

Done.

rive

★ please weld   part-1
                       part-3
                       Part-2

part-4

★ there is a gap
of 1mm. I need
this gap to pinch
something later.

★ please bend part-3
as follows the line of
part-1.

part-3   part-1

part-2

★ please weld from the bottom

To Axel Hintersel
Heel No.4

Masa please put th
into computer Kei

130

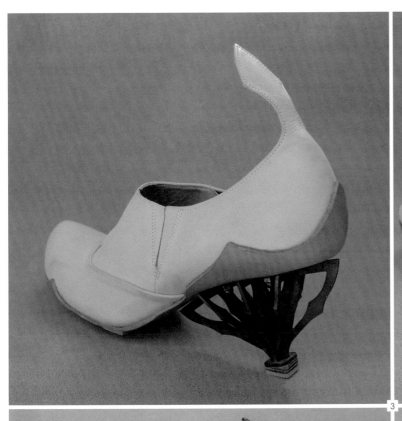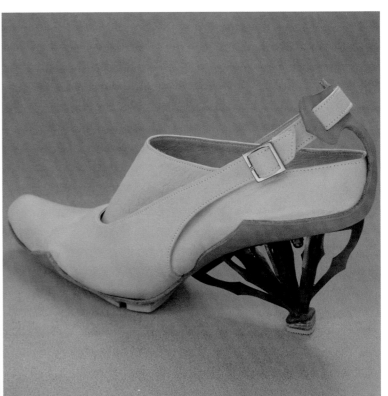

MEHER KAKALIA | LONDON, UK

www.meherkakalia.com

Photos © Vanessa Warren

1 DINALI, cow leather, Heel wood covered with leather, Sole leather with non-slip rubber outer, 2008

2 JAZZ, goat leather, Lining sheep leather, Heel wood covered with leather, Sole leather with re-cycled non-slip tyre, 2008

3 GRANADA, goat leather, Lining sheep leather, Heel wood covered with leather, Sole leather with re-cycled non-slip tyre, 2008

4 INGE, goat leather, Lining sheep leather, Klog Heel wood, Sole non-slip rubber, 2007

5 QUEEN Bee, metal coils embroidered on velvet, Lining sheep leather, Sole cow leather with 2 parts of crepe, 2005

6 RYU, Cow leather and salmon fish skin nose, Lining sheep leather, Heel wood covered with leather, Sole leather with non-slip rubber base, 2008

7 EMMA PEEL Boot, cow leather, Lining sheep leather, Sole cow leather, 2006

8 ANASTASIA, metal coils embroidered on velvet and leather trim, Lining Cow leather, Sole cow leather, 2008

Feral by Meher Kakalia mixes 500 year old techniques with modern styling. Kakalia, originally from Karachi, Pakistan, learned shoe making through local artisans. This led her to establish her own factory where she oversees her own production and employs local craftspeople to do embroidery that cannot be done with machines. She is keeping the sourcing and the manufacturing close to her heritage.

Meher Kakalias Label Feral verbindet 500 Jahre alte Techniken mit modernem Design. Kakalia stammt aus Karatschi in Pakistan, wo sie das Schuhmacherhandwerk bei einheimischen Handwerkern erlernte. Sie gründete schließlich ihren eigenen Betrieb, in dem sie die Produktion beaufsichtigt und lokale Kunsthandwerker für das Anfertigen von Stickarbeiten, die nicht von Maschinen verrichtet werden können, beschäftigt. Bei Auswahl und Herstellung bleibt sie ihren Wurzeln treu.

La marca Feral de Meher Kakalia combina el diseño moderno con técnicas de confección de 500 años de antigüedad. La diseñadora de Karachi, Pakistán, aprendió a confeccionar zapatos de forma tradicional. Esto la llevó a fundar su propia empresa, donde actualmente supervisa la producción de sus creaciones y emplea a artesanos locales para realizar bordados imposibles de producir con máquinas. En cuanto a la selección de los materiales y la confección de sus diseños, esta artista se mantiene fiel a sus raíces.

La marque Feral de Meher Kakalia allie des méthodes vieilles de 500 ans au stylisme moderne. Originaire de Karachi au Pakistan, Kakalia apprit la cordonnerie auprès d'artisans locaux avant de fonder sa propre entreprise dont elle surveille la production. Ses employés sont des artisans qui se chargent des broderies que les machines ne peuvent effectuer. Que ce soit en matière de sourcing ou de fabrication, elle tient à préserver ce dont elle a hérité.

Il marchio Feral di Meher Kakalia unisce tecniche consolidate da ormai 500 anni con uno stile moderno. Nata a Karachi, in Pakistan, Kakalia studiò l'arte di confezionare calzature dagli artisti locali. Ciò l'ha spinta a fondare la propria azienda in un luogo in cui lei stessa possa dirigerla, commissionando ad artigiani del posto lavori di ricamo impossibili da realizzare con le macchine. In questo modo resta fedele alle proprie origini con la scelta del luogo di provenienza e confezionamento delle sue scarpe.

1

3

2

4

5

6

8

KAORU KANEKO | VIGEVANO, ITALY

www.kanekodesign.it

Photos © Kaneko Design

1 One-Piece 2, White full-grain calf moccasin, SS 2004
2 One-Piece 7B, Group of pony skin moccasins in various colours, AW 2007
3 One-Piece 2, Group of BATIK stamped full-grain calf moccasin, SS 2005
4 One-Piece 0, Group of vegetable tanned calf mule, SS 2007
5 One-Piece 4, White full-grain calf short boots moccasin, AW 2004 (inside)
6 One-Piece 4, White full-grain calf short boots moccasin, AW 2004

Japanese born Kaoru Kaneko graduated from TAMA Art University Japan in Industrial design. He has since moved to Vigevano, to the heart of Italian footwear production to design and oversee his label. His beautifully crafted moccasins are made with a patented One-Piece system from the highest quality raw materials. The end result is clean and minimal.

Der in Japan geborene Kaoru Kaneko studierte Industriedesign an der TAMA Kunsthochschule in Tokio. Danach ging er nach Vigevano, ins Herz der italienischen Schuhproduktion, um sein Label zu entwickeln und zu managen. Seine wunderschön von Hand gefertigten Mokassins werden nach einem patentierten Ein-Stück-System und unter Verwendung hochwertigster Werkstoffe hergestellt. Das Ergebnis zeichnet sich durch Makellosigkeit und Minimalismus aus.

Kaoru Kaneko, de origen japonés, se graduó en diseño industrial en la TAMA Art University de Japón. Más tarde se mudó a Vigevano, corazón de la producción del calzado italiano, para crear y dirigir su propia marca. Sus mocasines, de maravillosa elaboración artesanal, están fabricados con un sistema patentado a partir de una sola pieza y con materiales de la más alta calidad. El resultado desprende un aire limpio y minimalista.

Né au Japon, Kaoru Kaneko est titulaire d'un diplôme de design industriel de l'université des beaux-arts TAMA à Tokyo. Depuis, il a déménagé à Vigevano, cœur de la production de chaussures en Italie, où il dessine et gère son label. Pour ses mocassins joliment faits à la main et titulaires du brevet One-Piece, il a recours à des matières premières de la plus haute qualité. Pour un résultat final propre et minimaliste.

Il giapponese Kaoru Kaneko studiò design industriale presso l'Università d'Arte TAMA di Tokio. Successivamente si trasferì a Vigevano, nel cuore dell'industria della calzatura italiana, per fondare e sovrintendere al suo marchio. I suoi mocassini, vere e proprie opere d'arte, sono realizzati con un sistema brevettato a un solo pezzo utilizzando materiali di altissima qualità. Il risultato finale è pulito e lo stile minimalista.

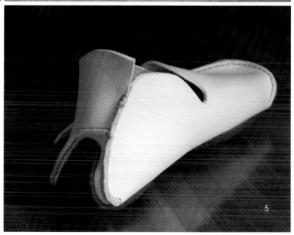

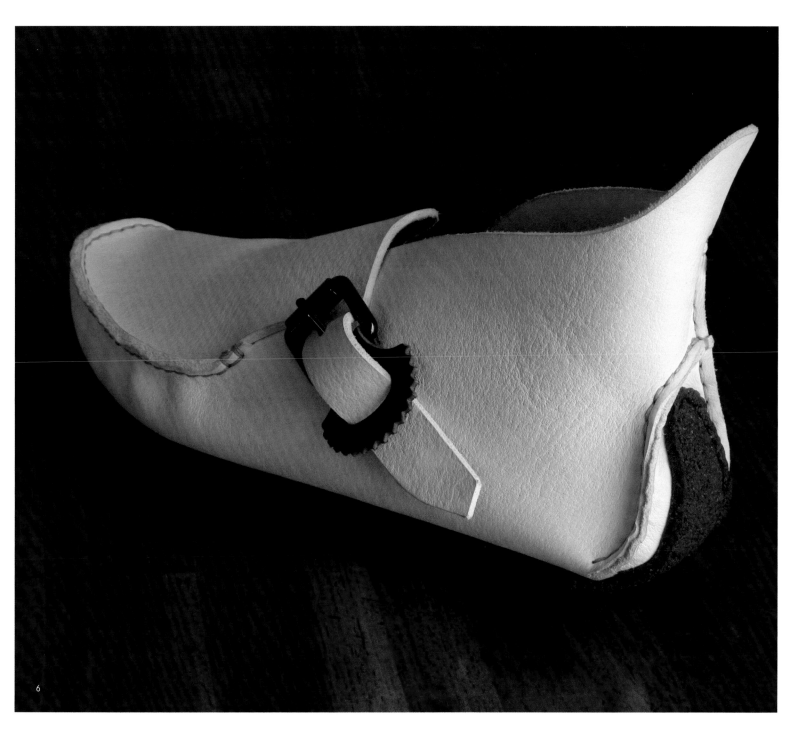

6

MAX KIBARDIN | MILAN, ITALY

www.maxkibardin.com

Photos © Max Kibardin, Sergio Valente (portrait)

1 Marianna, metallic pink blush nappa sandal with wine
   kid criss-cross draping detail, AW 2008
2 Franca, water green craquelet metallic nappa sandal,
   with dragonfly motif, SS 2008
3 Simonetta, pink suede pump with floral black patent
   Emile Galle motif, AW 2007
4 Samantha, wide heel violet quilted kid peep toe dorsay,
   AW 2008
5 Alessandra, peep toe ankle strap metallic chocolate
   nappa sandal, AW 2008
6 Alessandra, peep toe ankle strap cyclamen quilted
   nappa sandal, AW 2008
7 Franca, multicolor suede sandal, with dragonfly motif,
   SS 2008
8 Madlene, cyclamen suede cut-out shoe bootie with cut-
   out heel, AW 2008

Kibardin started his luxury footwear collection in 2005 and has been creating quite a stir with his combinations of color and exotic materials giving a unique sense of luxury. Kibardin takes inspiration from the world around him, details as diverse as Buddhist drapery, women's cosmetics and the insect world. Currently footwear consultant to many global brands, Kibardin is a definite rising star.

Max Kibardin debütierte mit seiner Luxusschuh-Kollektion 2005. Seine Kombinationen aus Farbe und exotischen Materialien, die ein einzigartiges Gefühl von Luxus vermitteln, sorgten für Aufregung. Kibardins Inspirationsquelle ist die Welt um ihn herum; dazu gehören so unterschiedliche Dinge wie buddhistische Textilien, Kosmetik für Frauen und die Welt der Insekten. Zurzeit ist Kibardin in beratender Funktion für viele internationale Marken tätig, was ihn endgültig zu einem aufsteigenden Star werden lässt.

Max Kibardin lanzó su primera colección de zapatos de lujo en 2005 y, desde entonces, ha causado bastante revuelo con sus creaciones, que mezclan diferentes colores y materiales exóticos de manera suntuosa. Este diseñador encuentra su inspiración en el mundo que le rodea, en motivos tan diferentes como las telas de estilo budista, los cosméticos para mujeres o el mundo de los insectos. En la actualidad asesora a numerosas marcas internacionales en temas de calzado y constituye, sin lugar a dudas, una de las nuevas promesas de la industria.

Max Kibardin débuta sa collection de chaussures de luxe en 2005. Entre-temps, ses combinaisons de couleurs et de matériaux exotiques créant un sentiment unique de luxe ont fait sensation. Kibardin s'inspire du monde qui l'entoure, de détails aussi variés que les tissus bouddhistes, la cosmétique pour femme et l'entomologie. Actuellement, Kibardin, véritable étoile filante, fait office de conseiller pour de nombreuses marques internationales.

Kibardin debuttò con la sua prestigiosa collezione di scarpe nel 2005, creando scompiglio per la sua combinazione di colore e materiali esotici che suggerisce un inconfondibile senso di raffinatezza. Kibardin trae ispirazione dal mondo che lo circonda, che può comprendere le cose più disparate come drappi buddisti, cosmetici femminili e il mondo degli insetti. Attualmente lavora come consulente nel settore della calzatura per numerose marche internazionali, il che gli spianerà sicuramente la strada verso il successo.

2

3

4

5

6

7

8

DAITA KIMURA | LONDON, UK

www.curiosityuk.com

Photos © PICZO

1 Big foot for smelly feet, 1994
2 Onion heel Boots & pumps, AW 2008
3 Gillie Boots, AW 2000
4 Twisted foot ball shoes, SS 2001
5 2-D sandal, AW 1999

Daita Kimura runs his label from one of the most charming and atmospheric retails spaces in the world: The 1567 building "The Old Curiosity Shop" immortalized by Charles Dickens. Daita was the creative force behind the Budhahood brand and has since shifted his focus onto his own designs that combine craft elements with often surreal detail.

Daita Kimura leitet sein Label von einer der bezauberndsten und stimmungsvollsten Verkaufsflächen der Welt aus: dem 1567 erbauten und durch Charles Dickens unsterblich gemachten „The Old Curiosity Shop". Daita Kimura war die kreative Kraft der Marke Budhahood, konzentriert sich nun aber auf seine eigenen Designs, in denen er Elemente des Kunsthandwerks mit häufig surrealen Details vereint.

Daita Kimura gestiona su propia marca desde uno de los locales comerciales más encantadores y cautivadores del mundo, el „The Old Curiosity Shop" (La Vieja Tienda de Curiosidades), un edificio construido en 1567 e inmortalizado por Charles Dickens en su novela del mismo nombre. Daita fue previamente la mente creativa tras la marca Budhahood. Desde entonces se ha concentrado en sus propios diseños, que combinan elementos artesanales con toques de aire surrealista.

Daita Kimura dirige son label depuis l'un des lieux de vente les plus charmants et poétiques du monde : « The Old Curiosity Shop », bâtiment construit en 1567 et immortalisé par Charles Dickens. Daita Kimura, jadis la force créative derrière la marque Budhahood, se concentre désormais sur son propre design qui marie des éléments issus de l'artisanat d'art et des détails souvent surréels.

Daita Kimura gestisce la sua griffe da uno dei punti vendita più suggestivi e affascinanti del mondo: "The Old Curiosity Shop", un edificio costruito nel 1567 e immortalato in una delle opere di Charles Dickens. Daita fu la mente creativa dietro la marca Budhahood, ma adesso si concentra solo sui suoi propri design, nei quali unisce spesso elementi di artigianato artistico con dettagli surreali.

2

3

4

5

NICHOLAS KIRKWOOD | LONDON, UK

www.nicholaskirkwood.com

Photos © Richard Stow

1 SS701, D-Ring Re-Wedge, Satin & Lizard with geometric laser-cut patent covered chopine motion re-wedge
2 SS827, D-Ring Sandal, Suede & Mirrored metallic with embossed suede & motion platform
3 SS805, Jet X Wrap Sandal, Satin with Swarovski fabric trim, motion platform & jet integral heel
4 AW822, Bound Buckle Sandal, Electric purple, "sueded" Alligator, calf trim with motion platform
5 AW801, Sunray Pleat Cut-out Sandal, Calf & Brocade with negative motion platform, sunray pleating & embroidery lace trim
6 SS828, X Wrap Sandal, Suede & Lizard with motion platform
7 AW821, Hi boot, Nubuck Alligator with demi-negative motion platform & gomma balance heel
8 AW814, Motion Court, Satin with motion platform & electric blue snake gomma balance heel
9 AW808, Fissure Bootie, Suede with demi-negative motion platform, embroidery lace slit trim, lizard gunmetal balance heel
10 SS809, Armour Sandal, Patent with mirrored metallic trim

Young British designer Nicholas Kirkwood has packed much into his short career. Launching his debut collection of architecturally inspired pieces in 2005 he has grown into an internationally acclaimed and recognised design talent, recently working with Chloé, Rodarte and Alberta Ferreti as well as accessories director for Pollini. Craftsmanship plays an integral role in all of Kirkwood's collections.

Der junge britische Designer Nicholas Kirkwood hat in seiner noch jungen Karriere bereits viel erreicht. Seine von der Architektur beeinflusste Debütkollektion kam 2005 auf den Markt. Seitdem ist er zu einem international gefeierten und anerkannten Designtalent geworden und hat kürzlich mit Chloé, Rodarte and Alberta Ferreti zusammengearbeitet, sowie als Accessories Direktor für Pollini. Kunstfertigkeit spielt in allen seinen Kollektionen eine wesentliche Rolle.

El joven diseñador británico Nicholas Kirkwood ha logrado mucho durante su relativamente corta carrera. En 2005 presentó su primera colección inspirada en la arquitectura. Desde entonces se ha convertido en un verdadero talento del diseño, muy solicitado y reconocido a nivel internacional. Actualmente trabaja con Chloé, Rodarte y Alberta Ferreti. La confección artesanal domina en todas sus colecciones.

Nicholas Kirkwood, ce jeune dessinateur britannique a déjà réussi de belles choses dans sa jeune carrière. En 2005, il débuta une collection inspirée de pièces architecturales. Talent très sollicité et mondialement reconnu par le secteur du design, il a récemment collaboré avec Chloé, Rodarte et Alberta Ferreti. L'artisanat fait partie intégrante de l'ensemble de ses collections.

Il giovane stilista inglese Nicholas Kirkwood ha già raggiunto molti traguardi nel corso della sua breve carriera. Dopo aver debuttato con la sua collezione di scarpe ispirate all'architettura nel 2005, è presto diventato uno stilista di grande talento riconosciuto a livello internazionale; di recente ha lavorato con Chloé, Zac Posen, Boudicca e Swarovski. La manifattura riveste un ruolo fondamentale in tutte le collezioni di Kirkwood.

2

3

4   5

8

9　　10

RUI LEONARDES | LONDON, UK

www.ruileonardes.com

Photos © Richard James

1 Men ankle boot MOD, Midnight blue patent leather,
   2006
2 Shoe / trouser all in one customized t-shirt DBC, leather,
   2007
3 Suit / shoe all in one OFFEND OFFEND OFFEND, Harris
   Tweed, Suede and leather, 2005
4 CHOCOLATE CAKE, Suede, 2004
5 Shoe / trouser all in one IGGY, Harris Tweed and Patent
   Leather, 2005
6 Shoe / trouser all in one, Offend Offend Offend, Wool,
   patent leather and embroidery, 2005

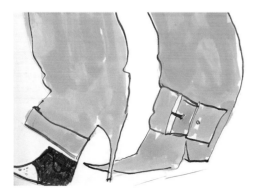

Azores born designer Rui Leonardes does not play it safe. His signature pieces are "trouser-shoes" that present a whole new silhouette for men. The collections cross gender boundaries and bring new ideas and dimensions to the otherwise safe menswear market. Rui Leonardes has a new vision for the future of men's dressing.

Der auf den Azoren geborene Designer Rui Leonardes spielt gerne mit dem Risiko. Seine charakteristischen Modelle sind „Hosen-Schuhe", die eine ganz neue Silhouette für Männer darstellen. Seine Kollektionen überschreiten die Grenzen zwischen den Geschlechtern und bringen neue Ideen und Dimensionen in den sonst so sicheren Markt der Herrenbekleidung. Rui Leonardes hat eine neue Vision für die Zukunft der Herrenmode.

Al diseñador Rui Leonardes, nacido en las islas Azores, le encanta el riesgo. Destacan sus „zapatos-pantalones", que presentan una silueta completamente innovadora para el hombre. Sus colecciones eliminan las fronteras entre sexos y aportan nuevas ideas y dimensiones al mercado de la moda masculina, donde se suele arriesgar poco. Rui Leonardes posee una visión diferente del futuro del vestuario masculino.

Née aux Açores, le dessinateur Rui Leonardes a le goût du risque. C'est à lui qu'on doit les « chaussures-pantalons », la présentation d'une toute nouvelle silhouette pour hommes. Ses collections ne s'arrêtent pas aux limites entre les sexes mais placent sur le marché de vêtements pour hommes, d'habitude si protégé, de nouvelles idées et dimensions. Rui Leonardes porte un regard novateur sur l'avenir de la mode masculine.

Nato nelle Azzorre, lo stilista Rui Leonardes è uno che ama il rischio. I suoi pezzi del tutto unici sono "scarpe-pantalone" che offrono agli uomini una silhouette completamente nuova. Le sue collezioni superano i confini tra di due sessi e portano nuove idee e dimensioni sul mercato altrimenti piuttosto omogeneo dell'abbigliamento maschile. Quella che propone Rui Leonardes è una nuova visione futuristica della moda uomo.

2   3

4

CHRISTIAN LOUBOUTIN | PARIS, FRANCE

www.christianlouboutin.com

Photos © Olivier Buhagiar

1 Very Noeud, yellow satin, SS 2008
2 Altadama, water snake, AW 2008 / 09
3 N°Privé, purple crocodile, SS 2008
4 Ron Ron, black patent, AW 2008 / 09
5 Armadillo, black leather, AW 2008 / 09
6 Pigalle, bleu sequin, SS 2008
7 Sacha, copper leather, SS 2008
8 Rodita, blue zipp, SS 2008
9 Anénome, plume satin and feathers, AW 2008 / 09

Born in Paris, Louboutin was enraptured by the high fashion and glamour of the dancehalls and clubs of 1970's Paris. Starting an apprenticeship with the Folies Bergère he went to work for Charles Jourdan and eventually Roger Vivier in 1988. He opened his flagship boutique in Paris in 1992 signalling the start of his brand of iconic and impossibly feminine styles. His designs are recognisable by their sensuous lacquered red soles.

Louboutin wurde in Paris geboren. Verzaubert von der Haute-Couture und dem Glamour in den Diskotheken und Clubs im Paris der 1970er-Jahre, begann er eine Ausbildung bei Folies Bergère, arbeitete für Charles Jourdan und 1988 schließlich für Roger Vivier. 1992 eröffnete er seine Flagship-Boutique in Paris – der Startschuss für eine Marke, die durch ungewöhnlich feminine Modelle mit Kultcharakter beeindruckt. Das besondere Kennzeichen seiner Schuhe sind die sinnlichen, rot lackierten Sohlen.

Louboutin se sintió cautivado por la alta costura y el glamour de los salones da baile y clubes del París de los años 70, su ciudad natal. Empezó su carrera como aprendiz en el Folies Bergère, más tarde trabajó para Charles Jourdan y finalmente, en 1988, para Roger Vivier. En 1992 inauguró su tienda principal en París, señalando así el inicio de su marca de estilos icónicos e increíblemente femeninos. Sus diseños son inconfundibles y se caracterizan por sus sensuales suelas lacadas en rojo.

Né à Paris, Christian Louboutin fut enchanté par la haute couture et le glamour des boîtes de nuits et des clubs dans sa ville natale des années 1970. Il entama une formation chez Folies Bergère, puis travailla pour Charles Jourdan et enfin pour Roger Vivier en 1988. En ouvrant sa boutique vitrine à Paris en 1992, il mit sur orbite sa marque au style iconique et hautement féminin. Trait particulier de ses réalisations : les semelles sensuelles vernies en rouge.

Affascinato dall'haute-couture e dal glamour delle discoteche e dei club della Parigi anni '70, Louboutin iniziò la sua formazione presso Folies Bergère, successivamente lavorò per Charles Jourdan e infine, a partire dal 1988, per Roger Vivier. Nel 1992 aprì la sua principale boutique a Parigi, sua città natale, segnando così l'inizio di una marca che, per il suo carattere estremamente femminile, è diventata uno status symbol. Segno distintivo delle sue scarpe sono le sensuali suole laccate di rosso.

2

3

5

6

7

8

9

FINSK | LONDON, UK
Julia Lundsten

www.finsk.com

Photos © Aleksi Niemela (1, portrait), Courtesy of Finsk (2, 3, 6), Max Oppenheim (4, 5)

1 Pleated peep-toe bootie, AW 2007 / 08
2 Graphic wooden heel platform, SS 2008
3 Graphic snake-skin wooden heel platform, SS 2008
4 Black / Bronze ankle boot with wooden Demi wedge, AW 2006 / 07
5 White / Bronze wooden heel ankle boot, AW 2006 / 07
6 Purple wooden heel sandal, SS 2008

Julia Lundsten is a Finnish-born London designer who has been dubbed the Eames of footwear. Her designs combine references to nature and Nordic architectural elements with an intellectual, yet humorous point of view. Lundsten likes to compare her shoes to a comfortable, yet well-designed chair, where her trademark wood heels are the legs and the upper is a seat for your foot; an elegant vessel to one of the most used parts of the body.

Julia Lundsten, Gründerin des Labels FINSK, wurde in Finnland geboren und arbeitet als Designerin in London. Sie gilt als der Eames der Schuhe. Ihre Designs vereinen Komponenten aus der Natur und architektonische Elemente Nordeuropas mit einer intellektuellen, dennoch humorvollen Auffassung. Lundsten vergleicht ihre Schuhe gerne mit einem gemütlichen, dennoch gut designten Stuhl, bei dem die für sie charakteristischen Holzabsätze die Beine darstellen und das Obermaterial ein Sitz für den Fuß ist - kurzum ein elegantes Behältnis für einen der aktivsten Teile des Körpers.

Julia Lundsten, fundadora de la marca FINSK, es una diseñadora de raíces finlandesas con residencia en Londres a la que se ha dado el apodo de la Eames del calzado. Sus diseños combinan referencias a la naturaleza con elementos de la arquitectura nórdica. Todas sus creaciones tienen un enfoque intelectual y divertido al mismo tiempo. A Lundsten le gusta comparar sus zapatos con una silla cómoda pero bien diseñada, en la que las patas serían sus característicos tacones de madera y la suela un asiento para el pie. Un elegante envoltorio para una de las partes más activas del cuerpo.

Née en Finlande, Julia Lundsten, la dessinatrice derrière la marque FINSK, vit maintenant à Londres. On l'appelle l'Eames de la chaussure. Elle mêle des dessins évoquant la nature et les éléments architecturaux de l'Europe du Nord à une interprétation aussi intellectuelle qu'hilare. Lundsten aime comparer ses chaussures à une chaise dont le confort ne se fait pas au détriment de la conception. Les typiques talons en bois en constituent les jambes tandis que la partie supérieure est un siège pour le pied - un récipient élégant pour l'une des parties du corps qui travaille le plus.

Julia Lundsten, fondatrice del marchio FINSK, nacque in Finlandia e lavora come stilista a Londra. Le sue creazioni, che le hanno procurato la fama di Eames delle scarpe, uniscono componenti della natura ed elementi architettonici dell'Europa settentrionale con una visione intellettuale e al contempo spiritosa. La Lundsten ama paragonare le sue scarpe a una sedia comoda e bella, della quale i tacchi in legno tipici dei suoi modelli rappresentano le gambe e la parte che racchiude il piede la seduta - insomma un elegante contenitore per una delle parti più utilizzate del nostro corpo.

2

2

3

3

NATACHA MARRO | LONDON, UK

www.natachamarro.com

Photos © Tony Rusecki (1, 4, 6), Natacha Marro (2, 3, 5), Claudio Scalas (portrait)

1 Mary-Jane polka dot leather platform
2 Open ankle boot with red transparent studs
3 Sailor oxford, electric blue nubuck shoe with white patent detail
4 Thigh high black rubber boots
5 Mock-crock, black oxford style shoe
6 Cream, burgundy and red knee high, lace-up burlesque boots

Natacha Marro grew up in Nice and now designs and runs her label from London. She opened her first shop in 2000 and has since worked with numerous TV and movie productions such as "Star Wars". Her hand making skills have also been noticed by the celebrity circuit and her towering heels are often seen on style icons such as Gwen Stefani.

Natacha Marro wuchs in Nizza auf und fertigt ihre Entwürfe nun in London an, von wo aus sie auch ihr Label leitet. Im Jahr 2000 eröffnete sie ihren ersten Laden und hat seitdem für viele Fernseh- und Filmproduktionen, wie z. B. „Star Wars" gearbeitet. Ihre Handarbeitsfähigkeiten blieben auch der Promi-Welt nicht verborgen; ihre Schwindel erregend hohen Absätze werden oft an Stilikonen wie Gwen Stefani gesichtet.

Natacha Marro creció en Niza y hoy diseña y dirige su propia marca desde Londres. Abrió su primera tienda en el 2000 y desde entonces ha colaborado en numerosos proyectos televisivos y cinematográficos, entre ellos „La Guerra de la Galaxias". Sus grandes dotes para la confección artesanal han llegado ya hasta el mundo de los famosos y sus tacones de vértigo adornan a menudo los pies de algunos iconos de la moda como Gwen Stefani.

Natacha Marro a grandi à Nice. Aujourd'hui, elle dessine et gère son label depuis Londres. En 2000, elle ouvrit sa première boutique. Depuis, elle a travaillé dans de nombreuses productions cinématographiques et télévisuelles telles que « Star Wars ». Ses compétences artisanales ne sont pas restées inaperçues dans le monde des célébrités comme en témoignent les talons vertigineux aux pieds de Gwen Stefani et d'autres icônes de style.

Natacha Marro è cresciuta a Nizza e ora disegna e gestisce la sua griffe a Londra. Aprì il suo primo negozio nel 2000 e da allora ha lavorato per diverse produzioni televisive e cinematografiche come per esempio "Guerre Stellari". La sua grande abilità di stilista delle calzature ha attirato l'attenzione anche di personaggi famosi: i suoi modelli con tacchi altissimi si vedono spesso ai piedi di icone dello stile come Gwen Stefani.

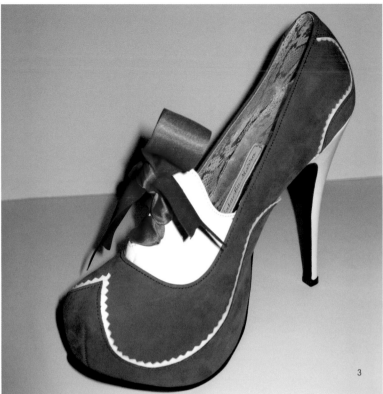

4

6

MARSU HOMME | SYDNEY, AUSTRALIA
Chrissy Hammond, Amy Low

www.marsuhomme.com

Photos © Jesus Manongdo (1, 2, 3, 6, 9, 10) Chrissy Hammond (4, 5, 7, 8)

1 Vince in Wax Grigo Perla Kangaroo, SS 2007
2 Patrick in Black Calf, SS 2008
3 Sam in White Napa, SS 2008
4 Alfred in Louvre Red Fox, SS 2007
5 Vince in Stonewash Black Brush Kangaroo, SS 2007
6 Vince Stonewash Black Kangaroo, Vince Wax Grigo Perla Kangaroo, Edward Wax Black Kangaroo, all SS 2007
7 Jimmy in Wax Black Kangaroo, SS 2007
8 Vince in Stonewash Black, pop up artwork by Benja Harney, SS 2007 Lookbook
9 Jesse in Black Calf, SS 2008
10 Benja in Tie Dye Black and White Kangaroo, SS 2007

Marsu Homme was established in 2004 by two friends Chrissy Hammond and Amy Low. The label is designed for the well travelled man and is made from interesting materials such as Kangaroo leather with shoes being made in Italy and Brazil. The brand brings sensitive and streamlined options to the men's fashion footwear market.

Marsu Homme wurde 2004 von den beiden Freundinnen Chrissy Hammond und Amy Low gegründet. Die Marke wendet sich an den vielgereisten Mann und verwendet interessante Materialien wie Känguruleder. Die Schuhe werden in Italien und Brasilien hergestellt. Das Label bringt anschmiegsame und stromlinienförmige Alternativen auf den Herrenschuhmarkt.

Marsu Homme fue fundado en 2004 por dos amigos, Chrissy Hammond y Amy Low. La marca está dirigida a un público cosmopolita masculino y sus creaciones están confeccionadas a base de materiales tan interesantes como, por ejemplo, el cuero de canguro. La fabricación y el acabado del calzado se llevan a cabo en Italia y Brasil. La marca aporta elementos de sensibilidad y dinamismo al mercado de la moda masculina.

Fondé en 2004 par les deux amies Chrissy Hammond et Amy Low, le label Marsu Homme s'adresse aux grands voyageurs. Il utilise des matériaux intéressants tels que le cuir de kangourou. La fabrication et la finition des chaussures se font en Italie et au Brésil. La marque apporte des options souples et profilées sur le marché de la chaussure pour hommes.

Marsu Homme fu fondata nel 2004 dalle due amiche Chrissy Hammond e Amy Low. La marca è pensata per uomini che hanno girato il mondo e utilizza materiali interessanti come la pelle di canguro. Le scarpe vengono confezionate e rifinite in Italia e Brasile. Questo nome porta sul mercato della calzatura maschile modelli dalle linee delicate e affusolate.

1

2

3

5

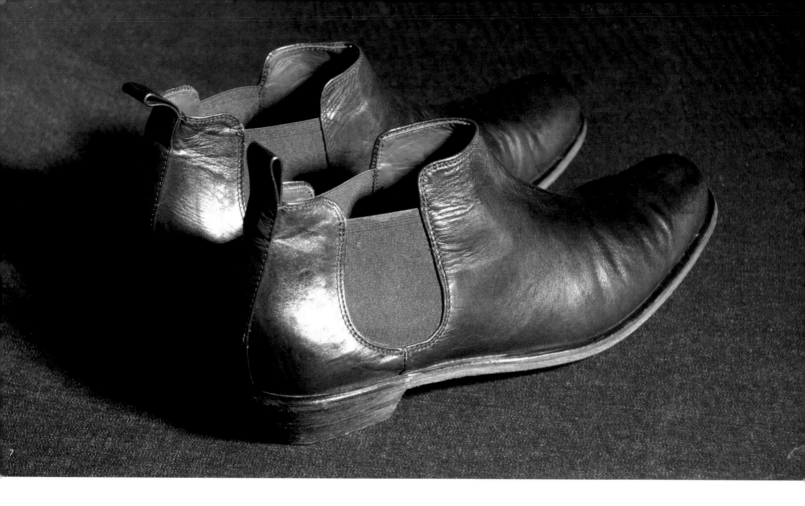

7

8

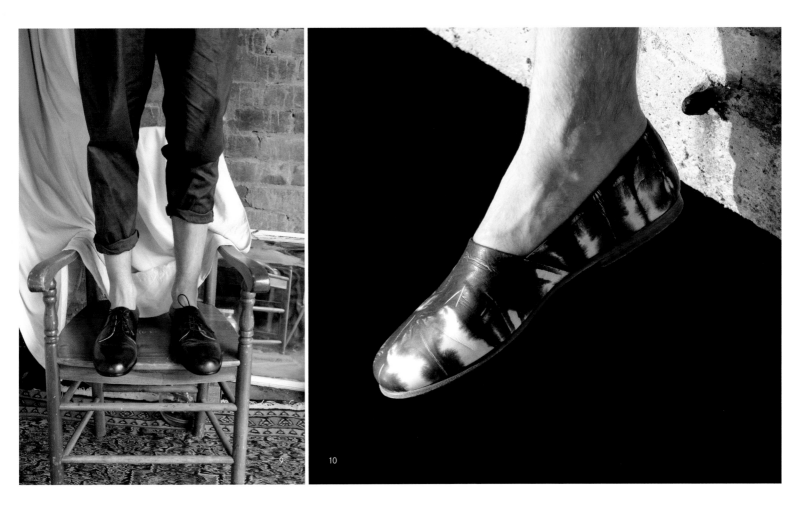

9

10

MATERIALBYPRODUCT | VICTORIA, AUSTRALIA
Susan Dimasi, Chantal McDonald

www.materialbyproduct.com

Photos © Sue Grdunac (1, 3, portrait), Paul Knight (2, 4-10)

1 Tattooed Derby, kangaroo leather, Tattooed Long Gaiter, kangaroo leather, Tattooed Glove Sleeves, kangaroo leather, wood, AW 2008 / 09
2 Tattooed Derby for Bjork, kangaroo leather, 2007
3 Tattooed Summer Derby, kangaroo leather, SS 2008, Tattooed Badges, kangaroo leather, bamboo, SS 2008
4 Tattooed Saddled Sleeve (flat), kangaroo leather, SS 2007
5 Tattooed Derby, kangaroo leather, SS 2007
6 Tattooed woven sleeves, kangaroo leather, SS 2007
7 Tattooed Saddled Sleeve, kangaroo leather, SS 2007
8 Tattooed Derby, Bjork Shoe, kangaroo leather
9 Tattooed Trainer, kangaroo leather, AW 2007 / 08
10 Tattooed Lace-Up Derby, Tattooed Long Gaiter, kangaroo leather, AW 2007 / 08

Launched in 2003 by Susan Dimasi and Chantal McDonald, MATERIALBYPRODUCT is a design studio working in an avant-garde manner by designing new ways for cutting, joining, marking and tailoring with a signature style that is both distinctive and unique. The design studio have made commissions for Björk and work in collaboration with footwear / designers Preston Zly and local tattoo artists Ben Ross and Kat Ratcliffe.

MATERIALBYPRODUCT wurde 2003 von Susan Dimasi und Chantal McDonald gegründet. Es handelt sich um ein Designstudio, das in einer avantgardistischen Weise neue Wege hinsichtlich des Zuschneidens, Zusammenfügens, Kennzeichnens und Schneiderns beschreitet und einen charakteristischen Stil entstehen lässt, der unverwechselbar und einzigartig ist. Das Studio hat bereits Aufträge für Björk ausgeführt und mit dem Schuhdesigner Preston Zly sowie den lokalen Tätowierungskünstlern Ben Ross und Kat Ratcliffe zusammengearbeitet.

En 2003, Susan Dimasi y Chantal McDonald inauguraron el estudio de diseño de planteamiento vanguardista MATERIALBYPRODUCT, donde se desarrollan maneras innovadoras de cortar, unir, marcar y coser con un estilo inconfundible y único. El estudio ha fabricado piezas por encargo para Björk y colabora en la actualidad con el diseñador de calzado Preston Zly y los artistas del tatuaje Ben Ross y Kat Ratcliffe.

Fondé en 2003 par Susan Dimasi et Chantal McDonald, MATERIALBYPRODUCT est une agence de design à l'état d'esprit avant-gardiste qui développe de nouvelles méthodes pour la coupe, l'assemblage, le marquage et la couture et signe ses réalisations de façon distinctive et singulière. Le studio a répondu à des commandes de Björk et coopère avec le dessinateur de chaussures Preston Zly ainsi qu'avec Ben Ross et Kat Ratcliffe, deux artistes de tatouage locaux.

Fondato nel 2003 da Susan Dimasi e Chantal McDonald, MATERIALBYPRODUCT è uno studio di design all'avanguardia che crea un nuovo modo di tagliare, assemblare, definire e confezionare le calzature distinguendosi per il suo stile del tutto particolare, per non dire unico. Lo studio ha realizzato scarpe per Bjork e collabora con lo stilista di scarpe Preston Zly e gli artisti locali del tatuaggio Ben Ross e Kat Ratcliffe.

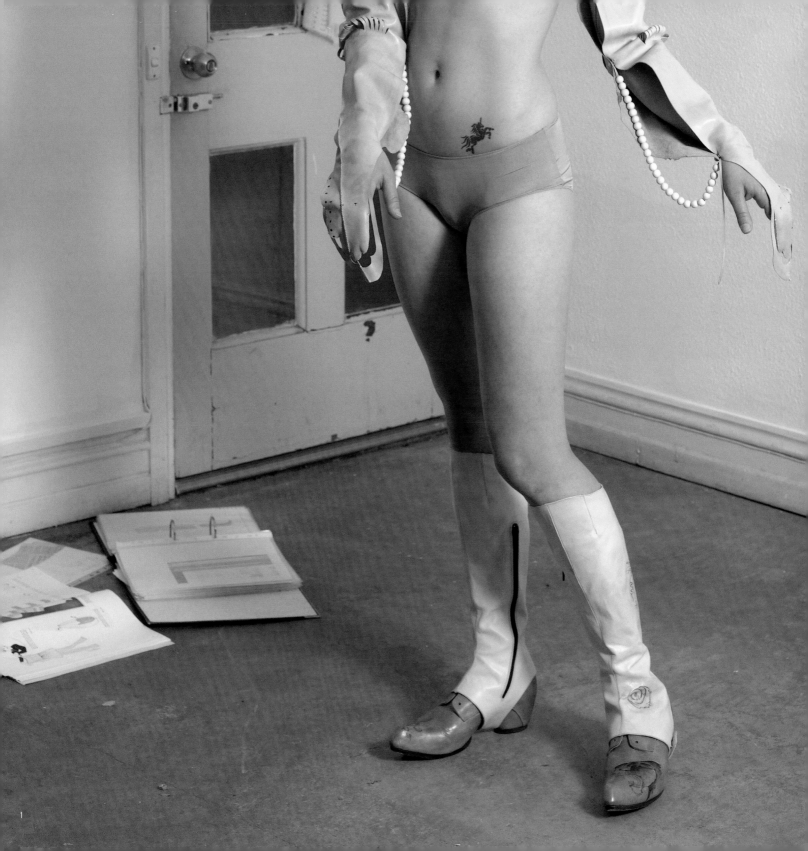

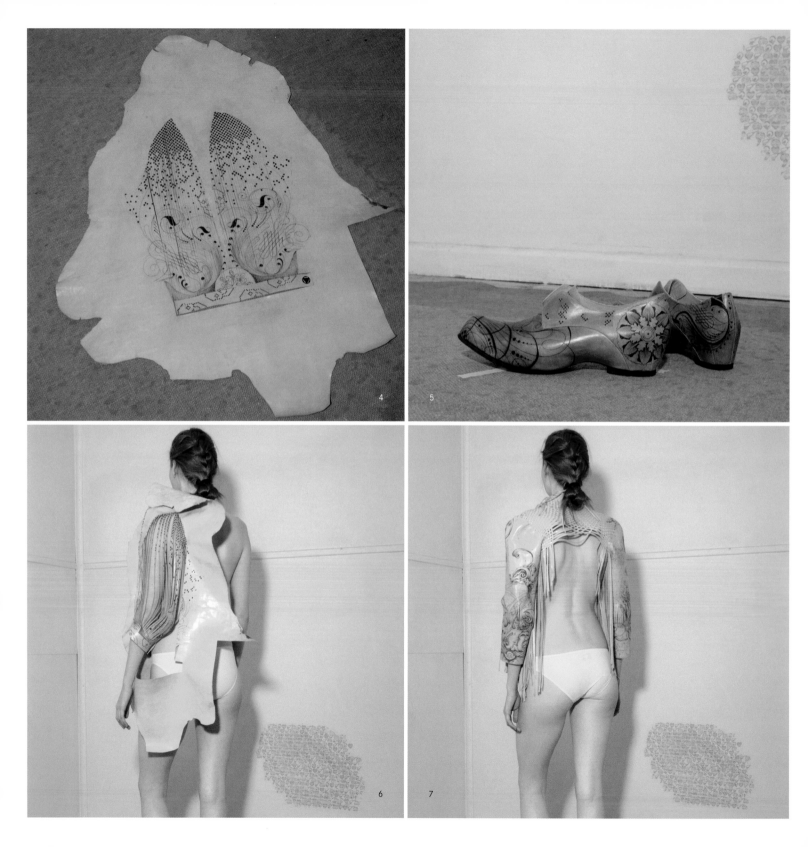

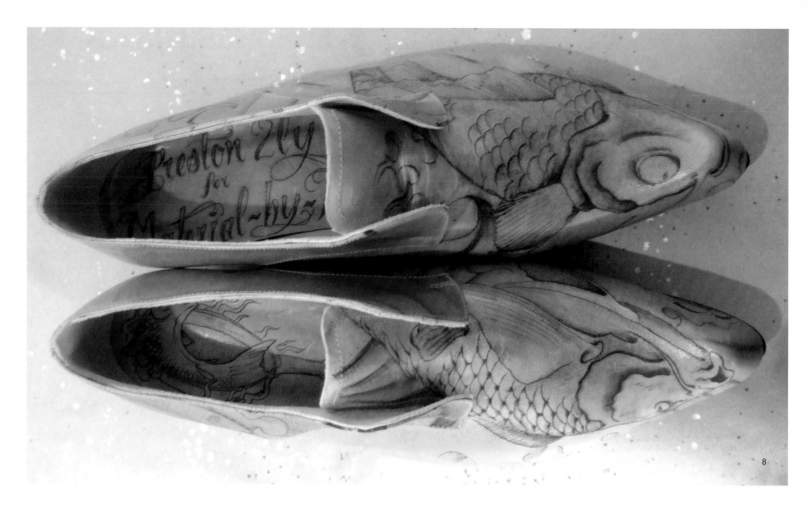

8

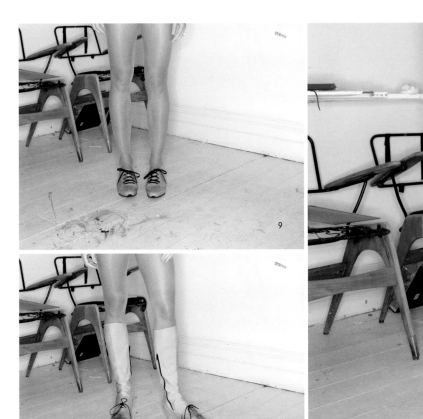

9

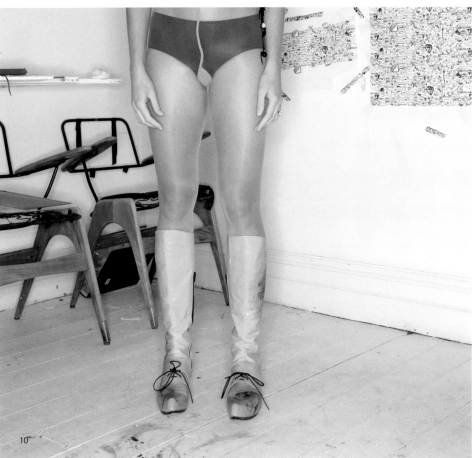

10

GIANNA MELIANI | PONTEDERA, ITALY

www.giannameliani.it

Photos © Gianna Meliani

1 Butterfly sandal, SS 2008
2 T-bar sandal, SS 2007
3 satin pumps with swarovski crystalized heel,
   AW 2008-2009
4 high heel satin T-bar sandal with studs, and velvet bow,
   AW 2008-2009
5 suede patchwork peep-toe platforms with pyramid heel,
   AW 2008-2009
6 peep-toe ankle boot in suede with leather heel,
   AW 2008-2009
7 shoe-boots in sambuca with laminated nappa leather
   trimmings and heel, SS 2007
8 peep-toe ankle boot in Mascagni with nappa leather
   heel, SS 2008
9 slingback sandal in carta cioccolata with laminated
   nappa leather heel, SS 2008

Gianna Meliani was born into a shoe producing family. Her family's factory produced shoes for many international brands and she fondly remembers Manolo Blahnik working closely with makers on the factory floor. She felt the time was right to launch her own brand in 1985 which has become one of the most successful Italian brands.

Bei Gianna Meliani liegt das Schuhmacherhandwerk in der Familie. Der Betrieb ihrer Familie fertigte Schuhe für viele internationale Marken. Meliani erinnert sich gerne an Manolo Blahnik, wie er mit anderen Schuhmachern eng zusammen in der Fabrik auf dem Boden saß und arbeitete. 1985 war für sie schließlich der richtige Zeitpunkt gekommen, ihr eigenes Label ins Leben zu rufen, welches mittlerweile zu einer der erfolgreichsten italienischen Marken avanciert ist.

Gianna Meliani nació en el seno de una familia de confeccionadores de zapatos. La empresa familiar producía calzado para numerosas marcas internacionales y ella aún recuerda con cariño como Manolo Blahnik trabajaba en la planta junto a otros artesanos. En 1985 sintió que había llegado el momento de lanzar su propia marca, la cual se ha convertido ya en una de las firmas italianas de más éxito.

Gianna Meliani est issue d'une famille dont l'activité a toujours été la chaussure. L'entreprise familiale fabriquait des chaussures pour de nombreuses marques internationales. Gianna Meliani se rappelle au bon souvenir de Manolo Blahnik quand celui-ci travaillait aux côtés des cordonniers sur le sol de l'usine. En 1985, elle se sentit prête à lancer sa propre marque devenue entre-temps l'un des plus célèbres labels italiens.

Per Gianna Meliani l'arte di confezionare scarpe è un dono ereditato: l'azienda della sua famiglia produceva già scarpe per molte firme internazionali, e lei ricorda con affetto come Manolo Blahnik, lavorasse seduto sul pavimento della fabbrica gomito a gomito con altri calzolai. Nel 1985 Gianna sentì che era arrivato il momento di dare vita alla sua marca personale, che nel frattempo è diventata una delle griffe italiane di più grande successo.

2

3

4

5

6

8

9

CHIE MIHARA | ALICANTE, SPAIN

www.chiemihara.com

Photos © Vicente Esteban

1 blue petrol pump with origami ornament, AW 2008 / 09
2 platform sandal with wide strap, coloured toplift,
  SS 2008
3 wide metalic strap, rectangular toe shape and banana
  stacked heel, AW 2008 / 09
4 small platform peep toe sandal, Laser work on upper,
  SS 2008
5 pump with over mixed colours, SS 2008
6 suede elastic boot with coloured toplift, AW 2008 / 09
7 T strap with cut outs, blue pipping around brown upper,
  blue banana heel, AW 2008 / 09
8 red woven open back pump, SS 2008
9 crocodile embossed brown peep toe T-strap with brown
  pipping all around shoe, AW 2008 / 09
10 red suede pump with rose ornament, AW 2008 / 09
11 crocodile embossed green peep toe T-strap with brown
  pipping all around shoe, AW 2008 / 09

Born in Brasil of Japanese parents, Mihara lived in Japan and New York before settling in Europe. She worked for Charles Jourdan before launching her own extremely successful brand in 2001. Design, comfort and quality are key to Mihara's designs which always feature carefully thought out details in a range of delectable colors and vintage inspired styles.

Als Kind japanischer Eltern in Brasilien geboren, lebte Mihara zunächst in Japan und New York, bevor sie nach Europa kam. Sie arbeitete für Charles Jourdan bevor sie 2001 schließlich ihre eigene, äußerst erfolgreiche Marke herausbrachte. Design, Komfort und Qualität sind die Grundpfeiler ihrer Arbeiten, die sich durch sorgfältig ausgewählte Details in einer Palette ansprechender Farben sowie durch von Vintage-Elementen beeinflusste Modelle auszeichnen.

Nacida en Brasil y de padres japoneses, Mihara vivió en Japón y Nueva York antes de instalarse en Europa. Antes de lanzar su propia y exitosa marca en 2001, trabajó para Sam & Libby y Charles Jourdan. Las obras de Mihara están caracterizadas por el diseño, el confort y la calidad, y destacan, sobre todo, por los detalles cuidadosamente escogidos en gamas de encantadores colores y estilos de inspiración vintage.

Fille de parents japonais, Chie Mihara naquit au Brésil, partit vivre au Japon et à New York et s'installa finalement en Europe. Elle travailla pour Sam & Libby et Charles Jourdan avant de lancer en 2001 sa propre marque à succès. Design, confort et qualité, voilà ce qui résume ses œuvres qui se caractérisent par des détails soigneusement sélectionnés et disponibles dans une gamme de couleurs attrayantes ainsi que par des modèles inspirés du vintage.

Nata in Brasile da genitori giapponesi, Mihara visse in Giappone e a New York prima di stabilirsi in Europa. Dopo aver lavorato per Sam & Libby e Charles Jourdan, nel 2001 esordì con la sua famosissima marca. Design, comfort e qualità sono i pilastri su cui poggiano i suoi lavori, che mettono invariabilmente in risalto dettagli scelti con cura e realizzati in una vasta gamma di colori delicati e stili ispirati al vintage.

2

3

4

5

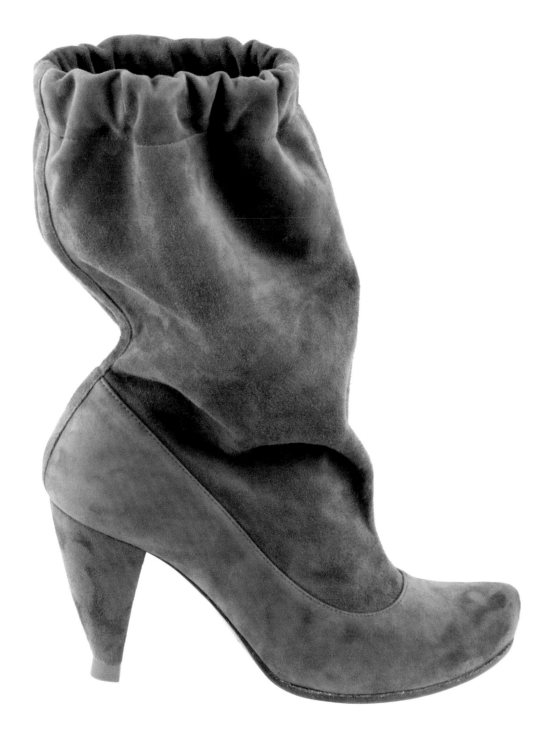

6

7

8

9

10

11

YUJI MIURA | MILAN, ITALY

miyuji@hotmail.com

Photos © KUMIKO IMATA

1 Derby, vegetable tanned calfskin
2 Oxford, with "open seamded" toe cap
3 Monk Strap, SS 2008
4 Oxford, suede counter as trainer detail

Japanese born Miura decided to make Italy his base for his footwear label. Previously working with Premiata and D&G he decided to launch on his own with collections that follow very clean lines with interesting, often surprising details. The shoes are carefully crafted in Italy from very high quality raw materials. The end result is timeless menswear that mixes Italian sophistication with Japanese sensibilities.

Der in Japan geborene Yuji Miura hat Italien als Ausgangsbasis für sein Schuhlabel gewählt. Zunächst arbeitete er für Premiata und D&G, beschloss dann aber, seine eigenen Kollektionen auf den Markt zu bringen. Diese zeichnen sich durch sehr klare Linien und interessante, oft überraschende Details aus. Die Schuhe werden mit großer Sorgfalt in Italien gefertigt, wobei qualitativ hochwertige Rohmaterialien verwendet werden. Das Ergebnis sind zeitlose Modelle für Männer, eine Mischung aus italienischer Raffinesse und japanischem Feingefühl.

El diseñador japonés Yuji Miura decidió ubicar en Italia el centro de operaciones de su marca de calzado. Después de trabajar algún tiempo con Premiata y D&G presentó sus propias colecciones, que siguen líneas muy claras y que a menudo incorporan detalles sorprendentes. Sus zapatos se fabrican en Italia y están elaborados con materiales de la más alta calidad. El resultado final es un calzado masculino a prueba de tiempo que fusiona la sofisticación italiana con la sensibilidad japonesa.

Né au Japon, Yuji Miura décida de gérer son label depuis l'Italie. Il avait travaillé avec Premiata et D&G avant de lancer ses propres collections qui se caractérisent par des lignes claires et des détails intéressants, voire surprenants. Les chaussures sont confectionnées en Italie avec délicatesse à partir de matériaux bruts de la plus haute qualité. Résultat : des modèles indémodables pour homme mêlant sophistication italienne et sensibilité japonaise.

Nato in Giappone, Miura ha scelto l'Italia come base per la sua marca di scarpe. Inizialmente lavorò per la griffe Premiata e D&G, ma poi decise di lanciare sul mercato le proprie collezioni, caratterizzate da linee molto chiare e tocchi interessanti, se non addirittura sorprendenti. Le scarpe vengono confezionate in Italia in modo molto accurato con l'impiego di materiali di altissima qualità. Il risultato finale sono calzature maschili senza tempo che mettono insieme raffinatezza italiana e sensibilità giapponese.

NAME: YUJI MIURA
PRODUCT: 2008-SS
SHOE: UTILITY, MAN'S
BASE MATERIAL: LEATHER
PRODUCED IN ITALY

NAME: YUJI MIURA
PRODUCT: 2008-SS
SHOE: UTILITY, MAN'S

2

2

3

3

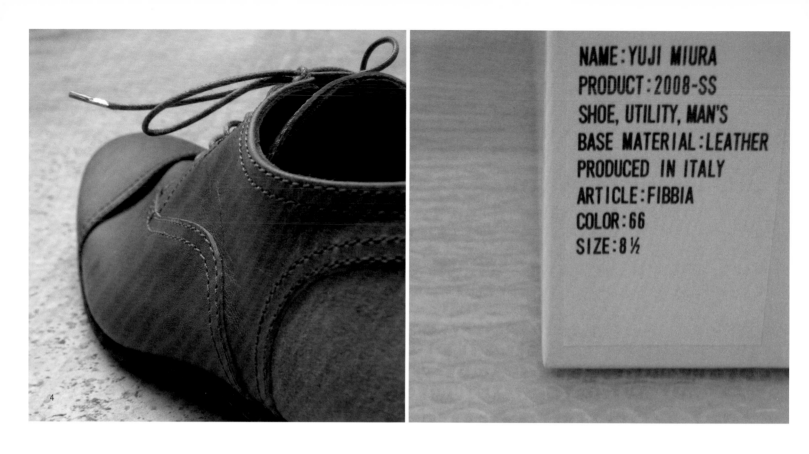

NAME:YUJI MIURA
PRODUCT:2008-SS
SHOE, UTILITY, MAN'S
BASE MATERIAL:LEATHER
PRODUCED IN ITALY
ARTICLE:FIBBIA
COLOR:66
SIZE:8½

4

EELKO MOORER | LONDON, UK

www.eelkomoorer.com

Photos © Ingrid Hora (1), Richard James (2, 3),
Bernadette Deddens (p 237), Barend Van Herpe (4)

1 Stilts, wood and clothe, 2003
2 Batshoes, Leather and wood, 2005
3 Leather Stilts, leather and metal, 2003
4 Wellies, Natural rubber latex, 2002

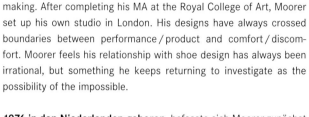

Netherlands born Moorer studied 3D design followed by shoe making. After completing his MA at the Royal College of Art, Moorer set up his own studio in London. His designs have always crossed boundaries between performance / product and comfort / discomfort. Moorer feels his relationship with shoe design has always been irrational, but something he keeps returning to investigate as the possibility of the impossible.

1976 in den Niederlanden geboren, befasste sich Moorer zunächst mit 3-D-Design und Schuhhandwerk, bevor er sein eigenes Atelier aufbaute. Nach seinem Master-Abschluss am Royal College of Art entschied sich Eelko Moorer in London zu bleiben und seine Designkarriere weiter voranzubringen. Seine Entwürfe überschreiten stets die Grenzen zwischen Performance und Produkt, Behagen und Unbehagen.

Nacido en Países Bajos en 1976, Moorer estudió diseño tridimensional y artesanía del calzado antes de abrir su propio taller. Después de terminar su master en el Royal College of Art, Eelko decidió quedarse en Londres para seguir avanzando en su carrera. Sus diseños han ido siempre más allá de los límites entre presentación-producto y comodidad-incomodidad.

Né en 1976 aux Pays-Bas, Eelko Moorer étudia le design 3D et la cordonnerie avant de monter son propre atelier. Après avoir obtenu son master au Royal College of Art, Moorer décida de rester à Londres et de poursuivre sa carrière dans le domaine du design. Ses dessins transgressent systématiquement les limites entre présentation et produit, aise et malaise.

Nato nel 1976 nei Paesi Bassi, Moorer inizialmente si occupò di design tridimensionale e artigianato delle calzature prima di inaugurare il suo atelier privato. Dopo aver concluso un master presso il Royal College of Art, decise di rimanere a Londra per portare avanti la sua carriera nel mondo del design. I suoi modelli si collocano sempre al confine tra prestazione e design, comfort e scomodità.

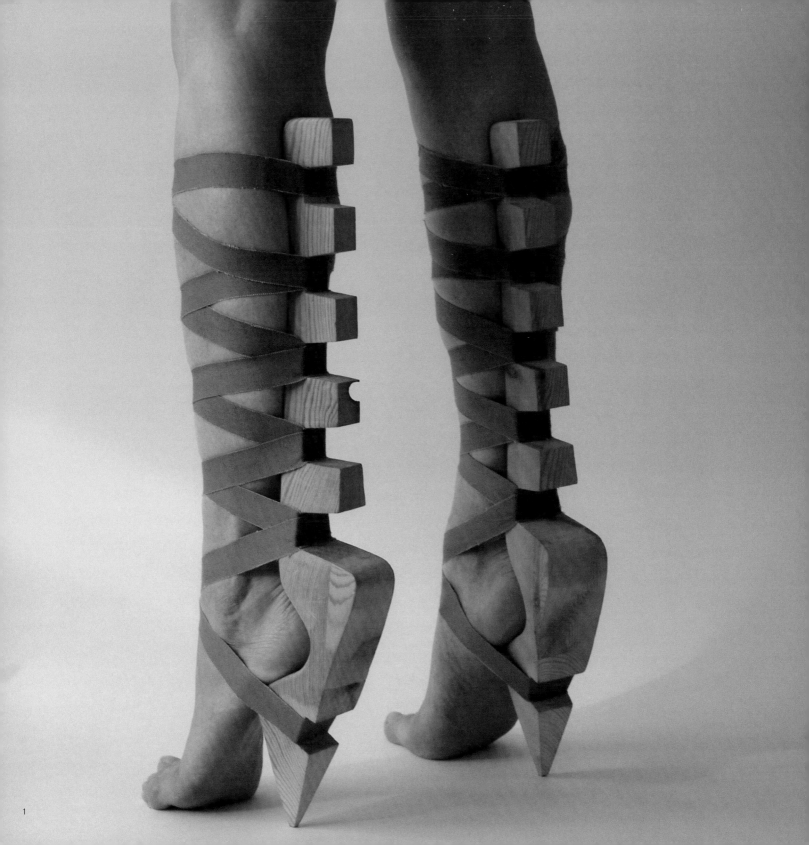

2

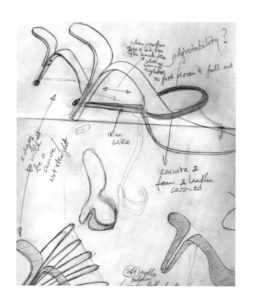

238

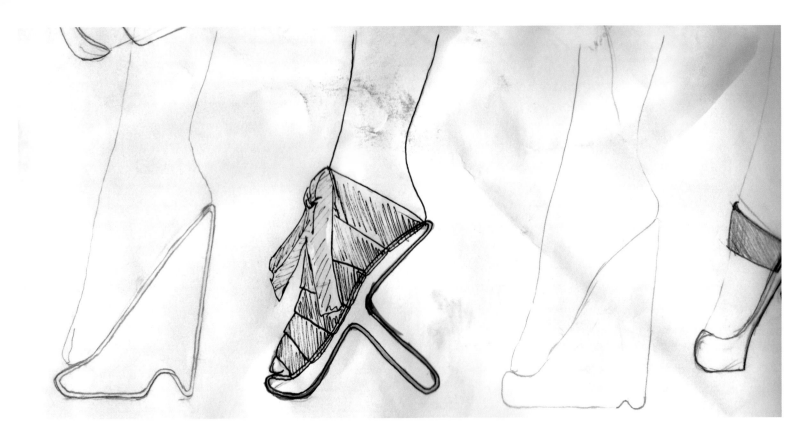

ANITA MOSER | SWITZERLAND

www.anitamoser.ch

Photos © buero:z (1-4, 6-9), Christian Knörr (5),
Emily Hautier (10-12)

1 Kinga (purple), Ogla (white), snakeskin, vegetably tanned
cowhide, SS 2005
2 Rorschach Big blot 1, Polyester fabric, Print, Leather
heel and thin platform sole, SS 2007
3 designing and developping process for collection
SS 2007
4 Rorschach, Small blot, Cowhide leather with laminated
upper, SS 2007
5 Rorschach Big blot 2, Polyester fabric, Cutted out patent
calf leather, Leather heel and thin platform sole,
SS 2007
6 Schnecke, Wiesel and Maulwurf, vegetably tanned cowhide, boxcalf, wooden heel, SS 2003
7 Semmelstoppel and Sunny Monday, waxed cotton or
Polyamid cord, moulded leather sole, kid leather,
SS 2004, SS 2006
8 Rainy Wednesday Night and Rainy Wednesday, waxed
linnen, kid leather, natural crepe sole, SS 2006
9 Sunny Monday, Polyamid cord, moulded leather sole, kid
leather, SS 2006
10 Andrej B., Boxcalf, Patent calf leather, vegetably tanned
cowhide, rubber sole, AW 2008 / 09
11 Konstatin T., vegetably tanned cowhide, waxed suede
leather, Patent calf leather, rubber sole, AW 2008 / 09
12 Eugen O., cowhide, waxed suede leather, Patent calf
leather, rubber sole, AW 2008 / 09

Anita Moser launched her footwear collection in 2003. Her style
combines hand crafted elements mixed with industrial design solu-
tions. The shoes have a very strong and robust feel but still carry
themselves with elegance. She has also now introduced a men's
collection to her label.

Anita Moser lancierte ihre Schuhkollektion 2003. Ihr Stil vereinigt
handwerkliche Details mit innovativen Designlösungen. Ihre Schuhe
sind gleichzeitig chic und spröde, elegant und robust. In Kürze wird
sie unter ihrem Label auch eine kleine, feine Herrenkollektion auf
den Markt bringen.

Anita Moser lanzó su primera colección de zapatos en 2003. Su
estilo combina elementos de confección artesanal con otros de
diseño industrial. Sus zapatos son fuertes y resistentes sin prescindir de la elegancia. La diseñadora acaba de presentar también una
colección para hombres.

Anita Moser débuta sa collection de chaussures en 2003. Son
style allie des éléments d'artisanat et de design industriel. Fortes et
robustes au toucher, ses chaussures demeurent néanmoins élégantes. Par ailleurs, elle vient de doter sa marque d'une collection pour
hommes.

Anita Moser lanciò la sua collezione di scarpe nel 2003. Il suo stile
combina elementi realizzati a mano con soluzioni di design industriale. I suoi modelli sono di fattura forte e robusta, ma risultano
tuttavia eleganti. Oggi la sua griffe comprende anche una collezione
di calzature per uomo.

2

3

4

5

9

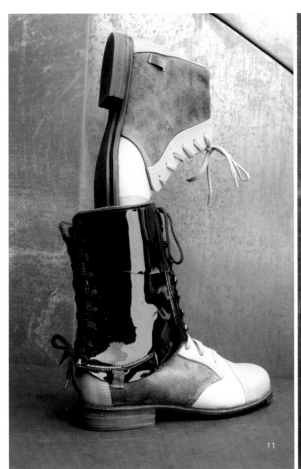

11

12

TRACEY NEULS | LONDON, UK

www.tn29.com

Photos © Uli Schade

1 pink rihno, nappa, 2006
2 orange envelope fastener, capri, 2004
3 essential ankle boots, patent pigskin, 2007
4 interweave flatty, hand woven nappa, 2006
5 egg holder peep toe, perforated capri, 2005
6 burn baby burn, sliced black calf, 2008

Born in Canada, the London-based designer Tracey Neuls started women's footwear brand TN_29 in 2000 launching TRACEY NEULS in recent years. Her decision to make the wearer's individuality and comfort top priority has made her the creative individual's favourite footwear designer and set her aside from her peers. Much more than just containers for your feet, Neuls' shoes are timeless expressions of individuality and a mark of the wearers fashion confidence.

Die in Kanada geborene, nun in London lebende Designerin Tracey Neuls gründete 2000 die Damenschuhmarke TN_29; vor einigen Jahren folgte das Label TRACEY NEULS. Ihr Entschluss, die Individualität der Trägerin und Komfort zu ihrer höchsten Priorität zu machen, ließ sie bei kreativen Personen zur beliebtesten Schuhdesignerin werden und unterscheidet sie von ihren Kollegen. Neuls' Schuhe sind viel mehr als nur eine Hülle für die Füße, nämlich zeitloser Ausdruck von Individualität und Zeichen des modischen Selbstvertrauens der Trägerin.

Tracey Neuls nació en Canadá y trabaja hoy desde Londres. En 2000 lanzó su marca de calzado para mujeres TN_29, a la que ha añadido, en los últimos años, la marca TRACEY NEULS. Su decisión de anteponer la individualidad y el confort en sus creaciones le ha dado el status de diseñadora favorita entre las mentes creativas y la ha distinguido de la competencia. Los zapatos de Neuls son mucho más que meros recipientes para los pies; son más bien una expresión atemporal de individualidad y una prueba del compromiso con la moda por parte de quien los calza.

Née au Canada, la dessinatrice Tracey Neuls vit maintenant à Londres. Elle lança sa marque de chaussures femme TN_29 en 2000. S'ensuivit tout récemment le label TRACEY NEULS. Résolue à donner la priorité à l'individualité et au confort de sa clientèle, elle est devenue la dessinatrice de chaussures préférée de ceux qui recherchent la créativité et se démarque de ses homologues. Ses chaussures font bien plus qu'entourer les pieds. Elles sont l'expression indémodable de l'individualité et illustrent toute l'assurance stylistique dont font preuve les personnes qui les portent.

Nata in Canada e attualmente residente a Londra, Tracey Neuls inaugurò la sua marca di scarpe per donna TN_29 nel 2000, mentre di recente ha lanciato la sua collezione TRACEY NEULS. La sua decisione di dare priorità assoluta al comfort e all'individualità dell'indossatrice ha fatto di lei la stilista di scarpe più amata dalle donne creative, permettendole così di distanziare i suoi colleghi. Le scarpe della Neuls sono molto più di una semplice protezione per i piedi: sono piuttosto espressioni senza tempo di individualità e un segno evidente che l'indossatrice si intende benissimo di moda.

3

4

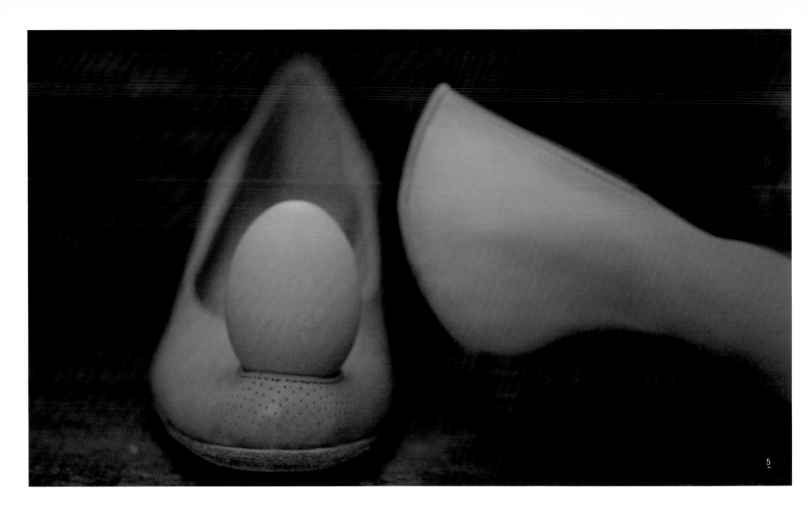

5

CHARLOTTE OLYMPIA | LONDON, UK
Charlotte Dellal

www.charlotteolympia.com

Photos © Alicia Taylor, Alice Dellal (portrait)

1 Piano shoe, black suede kidskin and black & white patent calfskin, AW 2008
2 Daphne shoe, blue velvet and black suede kidskin, AW 2008
3 Cindy shoe, grey and black suede kidskin with black patent calfskin tassel, AW 2008
4 Greta shoe, imitation ostrich skin, red stamped calfskin, AW 2008
5 Cindy Masako shoe, red suede kidskin, gold metallic calfskin and red satin, SS 2008

Charlotte Dellal, who designs the label 'Charlotte Olympia', studied at Cordwainers. After graduating in 2004 she designed a capsule collection of cork inspired pieces. Her spring / summer 2008 debut collection included ultra-elegant designs made from kimono fabrics inspired by the glamour of Forties Hollywood.

Charlotte Dellal, verantwortlich für das Label „Charlotte Olympia", studierte am Cordwainers College. Nach ihrem Abschluss im Jahr 2004, entwarf sie eine Sonderkollektion, bei der ihr Kork als Inspirationsquelle diente. In ihrer Debütkollektion Frühjahr / Sommer 2008 finden sich sensationell elegante Designs aus Kimonostoffen, inspiriert vom Hollywood-Glamour der 40er-Jahre.

Charlotte Dellal, egresada del instituto Cordwainers, está tras el diseño de la marca „Charlotte Olympia". En 2004, después de terminar sus estudios, diseñó una colección cápsula de artículos inspirados en corcho. Su colección debut primavera / verano de 2008 incluye diseños extremadamente elegantes fabricados con telas de kimono e inspirados en el glamour hollywoodiano de los años cuarenta.

Charlotte Dellal, à qui l'on doit le label « Charlotte Olympia » fit ses études au Cordwainers. Après avoir décroché son diplôme, elle conçut une collection spéciale placée sous le signe du liège. Sa collection printemps / été 2008, celle de ses débuts, regroupait des designs ô combien élégants réalisés à partir de tissus kimono inspirés du glamour hollywoodien des années 40.

Charlotte Dellal studiò al Cordwainers College e ora lavora come stilista per la marca "Charlotte Olympia". Dopo la laurea nel 2004, disegnò una capsule collection di modelli ispirati al sughero. Nella sua collezione di esordio primavera / estate 2008 si riscontrano design ultra-eleganti realizzati con stoffe di kimono e ispirati al glamour della Hollywood anni '40.

2

3

4

5

BEATRIX ONG | LONDON, UK

www.beatrixong.com

Photos © Dean Chalkley (1-4), Charlotte Tolhurst (5)

1 Kim, wedge with ankle tie in indira silk, SS 2008
2 Taylor, patent platform with ankle tie in indira silk, SS 2008
3 Naomi, 3-strap peep toe platform in varnished red patent, SS 2008
4 Tori, peep toe platform in green patent, SS 2008
5 (L to R) Berkshire, lace-up platform in cigar leather; Hermos, over-the-knee boot in cigar leather; Roedean, round toe pump in grey wool felt; Cambridge, low wedge lace-up in tan leather and grey wool felt; Stowe, simple platform in grey wool felt; Berkshire, simple platform in grey wool felt; Glare, high-heel mary-jane in grey python; Cambridge, low wedge lace-up in tan leather and green cravate; Stowe, low wedge lace-up in tan leather and green cravate, AW 2008-2009

Launched in September 2002, Beatrix Ong has built an extremely successful luxury shoe brand creating unique, elegant and distinctive designs. Having worked for Jimmy Choo, Ong's experience translates excellently into wearable styles with a focus on comfort and stability whilst retaining elegance and finesse. Ong's expanding empire includes a flagship London store, and a private salon for her increasing list of private clients and celebrity fans.

Beatrix Ong brachte im September 2002 ihre Luxus-Schuhmarke auf den Markt, die sehr erfolgreich einzigartige, elegante und markante Designs vereint. Ongs Erfahrung – sie arbeitete u. a. für Jimmy Choo – zeigt sich hervorragend in ihren tragbaren Modellen, bei denen Komfort und Stabilität im Vordergrund stehen, während Eleganz und Finesse bewahrt bleiben. Ongs wachsendes Imperium umfasst zwei Läden in London und einen privaten Salon für die immer größer werdende Schar an prominenten Fans.

En septiembre de 2002, Beatrix Ong lanzó su propia y extremadamente exitosa marca de zapatos de lujo conjugando diseños únicos, elegantes e inconfundibles. Ong tuvo la oportunidad de trabajar para Jimmy Choo y hoy su experiencia se traduce en estilos tan cómodos como prácticos, basados en el confort y la estabilidad, pero sin renunciar a la elegancia y el refinamiento. Su creciente imperio incluye dos tiendas en Londres y un sala de muestras privada para sus admiradores más célebres, que también van en aumento.

Créée en 2002, Beatrix Ong est devenue une marque de chaussures de luxe à succès grâce à ses designs uniques, élégants et marqués. Pour avoir travaillé pour Jimmy Choo, son expérience se prête brillamment aux modèles portables où l'accent est mis sur le confort et la stabilité tout en préservant l'élégance et la finesse. En pleine expansion, l'empire d'Ong comprend deux boutiques à Londres et un salon privé destiné aux célébrités de plus en plus nombreuses à l'affectionner.

Dopo il suo debutto nel settembre 2002 Beatrix Ong ha riscosso un notevole successo nel mondo delle calzature realizzando una linea di lusso dai design unici, eleganti e decisi. Forte della sua esperienza lavorativa per conto di Jimmy Choo, oggi la Ong propone splendidi modelli facilmente indossabili che puntano sul comfort e la stabilità senza rinunciare a eleganza e finezza. Il suo crescente impero conta due negozi a Londra e un salone privato per i sempre più numerosi fan che la stilista annovera tra i personaggi famosi.

1

3

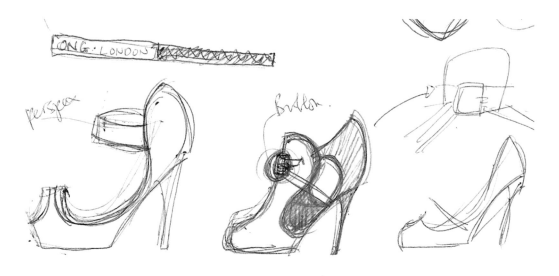

ONG·LONDON

perspex

button

MINNA PARIKKA | HELSINKI, FINLAND

www.minnaparikka.com

Photos © Nina Merikallio (1, 2, 5-7), Empa Rodriguez (3, 4), Saila Semeri (8-10), Jukka Rapo (portrait)

1 Grace, The Speakeasies collection, SS 2008
2 Morticia, The Speakeasies collection, SS 2008
3 Armi, Perfume collection, AW 2008-09
4 Marie, Perfume collection, AW 2008-09
5 Raquel, Priscilla and bag Maxine, Jealousy collection, AW 2007-08
6 Alexandra, Jealousy collection, AW 2007-08
7 Jackie, Susanna and Aili, Perfume collection, AW 2008-09
8 Morticia, The Speakeasies collection, SS 2008
9 Ruby, The Speakeasies collection, SS 2008
10 Elsa, The Speakeasies collection, SS 2008

Minna Parikka is a Finnish designer who studied footwear design at De Montfort University in Leicester. Now based in Helsinki, Finland, her shoes have a very strong individual voice that speaks clearly of the designer herself. Her designs have a distinctively vintage feel with influences from the turn of the 20th century to the glamorous 1950's influence with unquestionable contemporary sexiness for today's confident woman.

Minna Parikka ist eine finnische Designerin, die an der De Montfort University in Leicester Schuhdesign studierte und heute in Helsinki lebt. Ihre Schuhe sprechen eine sehr starke, individuelle Sprache, die ganz eindeutig auf die Designerin selbst verweist. Ihr Design ist unverwechselbar vom Glamour der 1950er-Jahre beeinflusst, gepaart mit unbestreitbarer, zeitgenössischer Sinnlichkeit für die selbstbewusste Frau von heute.

La diseñadora finlandesa Minna Parikka estudió diseño de calzado en la De Montfort University de Leicester. En la actualidad trabaja desde Helsinki, Finlandia, y todos sus zapatos ostentan un marcado carácter propio que refleja también la personalidad de la autora. Sus diseños poseen un inconfundible aire vintage con influencias de finales del siglo XX y el glamour de los años 50, mientras ofrecen un incuestionable toque sexy a la mujer moderna y segura de si misma.

Minna Parikka est une dessinatrice finlandaise qui étudia le design de chaussure à la De Montfort University à Leicester. Actuellement, elle vit à Helsinki. Ses chaussures ont un caractère fort et individuel. On voit là que c'est la dessinatrice en personne qui s'exprime. Ses dessins sont soumis à un accent traditionnel et aux influences de fin de siècle, mais s'inspirent également du glamour des années 1950 avec une sensualité incontestablement contemporaine pour la femme actuelle faisant preuve d'assurance.

Minna Parikka è una stilista finlandese che studiò design di scarpe presso la De Montfort University di Leicester e oggi abita a Helsinki. Le sue scarpe rivelano uno stile molto personalizzato che rimanda chiaramente al carattere della stilista stessa. I suoi modelli denotano un inconfondibile glamour anni '50 che si fonde con un'indiscutibile sensualità moderna pensata per il carattere sicuro della donna di oggi.

3

4

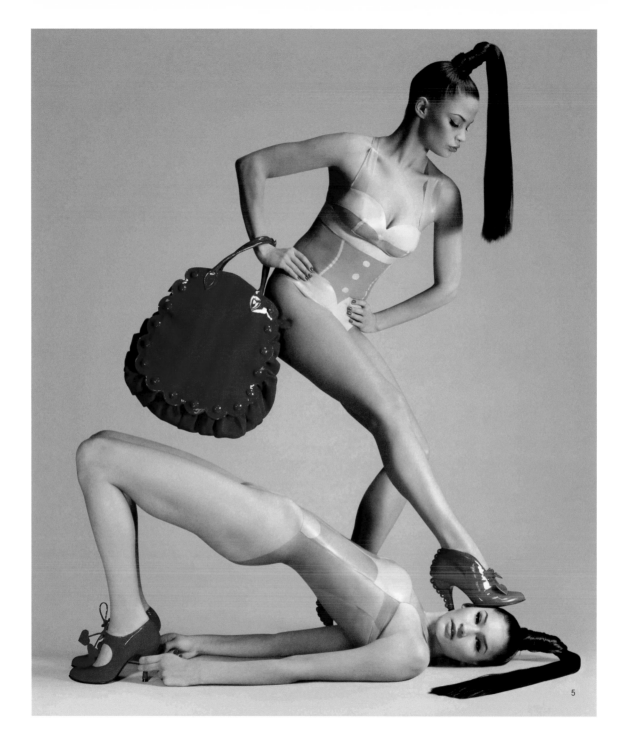

5

6

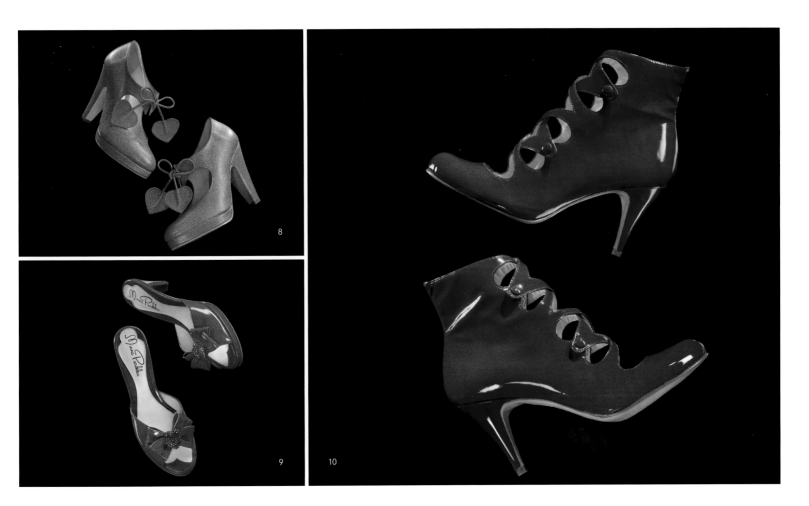

8

9

10

PREMIATA | MILAN, ITALY
Graziano Mazza

www.premiata.it

Photos © Jovanka Savic (1, 4, 5, 8, 9), Daniele Rossi
(2, 3, 6, 7), Frances Melhop (portrait)

1 Décolleté, grey kid leather, Décolleté with plateaux and
   peep toe black shiny kid leather, SS 2008
2 Lace up men shoe, black calf leather, SS 2008
3 Lace up women shoes, square perforated grey leather,
   Slingback sandal, plateau, peep toe, cream kid leather,
   SS 2008
4 Lace - up shoe, grey calf leather, AW 2008 / 09
5 Ankle boot, black cracklè leather "asphalt effect",
   AW 2008 / 09
6 Ankle boot, peep toe, pinstriped black calf leather,
   SS 2007
7 Lace - up shoes, old brown mat calf leather, SS 2007
8 Décolleté, rounded toe and satin stripe, black kid
   leather, AW 2008
9 Décolleté, plateau, slightly open toe, two - tones inter-
   weawe calf leather, SS 2008

Premiata was created in 1995 by Graziano Mazza who wanted to take this long running family brand into new territories from traditionally classic to modern. His sharp designs are wearable yet experimental and have expanded to include three lines of shoes, an accessory collection and a prêt-à-porter clothing collection with a flagship boutique in Milan.

Das Label Premiata wurde 1995 von Graziano Mazza gegründet, mit der Absicht, die alte Familienmarke in neue Gewässer zu führen, von traditionell klassisch zu modern. Seine spitzen Designs sind tragbar, dennoch experimentell. Mittlerweile gibt es drei Produktlinien von Schuhen, eine Accessoire-Kollektion sowie eine Kollektion Prêt-à-porter-Kleidung mit einer Flagship-Boutique in Mailand.

Premiata fue creada en 1995 por Graziano Mazza, que quiso llevar esta tradicional empresa familiar a nuevos terrenos, logrando el salto de lo clásico y tradicional a lo moderno. A pesar de su carácter experimental, sus marcados diseños resultan también cómodos y prácticos. Mazza ha añadido además tres líneas de zapatos diferentes, una colección de accesorios y una colección prêt-à-porter al patrimonio de la empresa. La tienda principal se encuentra en Milán.

Premiata fut créée en 1995 par Graziano Mazza qui voulait redéfinir la marque familiale riche en tradition par le biais d'une transition du classique vers le moderne. Si on peut les porter, ses designs pointus sont toutefois expérimentaux. Ayant fait l'objet d'un élargissement, ils comprennent actuellement trois lignes de chaussures, une collection accessoire et une collection de vêtements prêt-à-porter avec un boutique vitrine à Milan.

La firma Premiata fu fondata nel 1995 da Graziano Mazza con l'obiettivo di rinnovare questo marchio familiare di lunga data portandolo dal classico al moderno. Le sue eleganti creazioni sono al contempo sperimentali e facilmente indossabili e ora comprendono tre linee di scarpe, una collezione di accessori e una di abbigliamento prêt-à-porter con una boutique principale a Milano.

4

5

8

9

KARIM RASHID | NEW YORK (NY), USA

www.karimrashid.com

Photos © Karim Rashid Inc., Milovan Knezevic (portrait)

1 Mirror, leather upper, Spring 2005
2 Cross, leather upper, Fall 2006 track line
3 Klack, leather upper, Spring 2006 cycle line
4 Moc, leather and elastic upper, Fall 2006 track line
5 Kick, leather upper, Spring 2006 cycle line
6 Kick, leather upper, Spring 2006 cycle line
7 Spider, leather and rubber upper, Spring 2004
8 Bondage, leather and rubber upper, Spring 2006 shell line
9 Conk, and rubber upper, Spring 2006 shell line

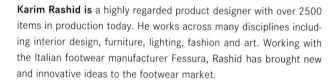

Karim Rashid is a highly regarded product designer with over 2500 items in production today. He works across many disciplines including interior design, furniture, lighting, fashion and art. Working with the Italian footwear manufacturer Fessura, Rashid has brought new and innovative ideas to the footwear market.

Karim Rashid ist ein hoch angesehener Produktdesigner mit heute mehr als 2500 Artikeln in Produktion. Er arbeitet in vielen Bereichen, darunter Innenarchitektur, Möbel, Beleuchtung, Mode und Kunst. In Zusammenarbeit mit dem italienischen Schuhfabrikanten Fessura hat Rashid neue und originelle Ideen auf den Schuhmarkt gebracht.

Karim Rashid es un reconocido diseñador, cuyo trabajo comprende actualmente más de 2500 creaciones en producción. Trabaja en diferentes disciplinas, incluyendo el diseño de interiores, muebles, iluminación, moda y arte. A través de su cooperación con la casa de calzados italiana Fessura, Rashid ha conseguido introducir nuevas e innovadoras ideas en el mercado.

Karim Rashid est un concepteur de produit très estimé dont la fabrication s'élève aujourd'hui à plus de 2500 articles. Il couvre plusieurs champs disciplinaires tels que le design intérieur, les meubles, l'éclairage, la mode et l'art. En coopération avec Fessura, fabricant de chaussures italien, Rashid a gratifié le marché de la chaussure d'idées nouvelles et innovatrices.

Karim Rashid è un designer altamente quotato di cui oggi si contano oltre 2500 articoli in produzione. Lavora in diversi campi come design di interni, arredamento, lampade, moda e arte. In collaborazione con il produttore italiano di calzature Fessura, Rashid ha arricchito il mercato delle scarpe con idee del tutto innovative.

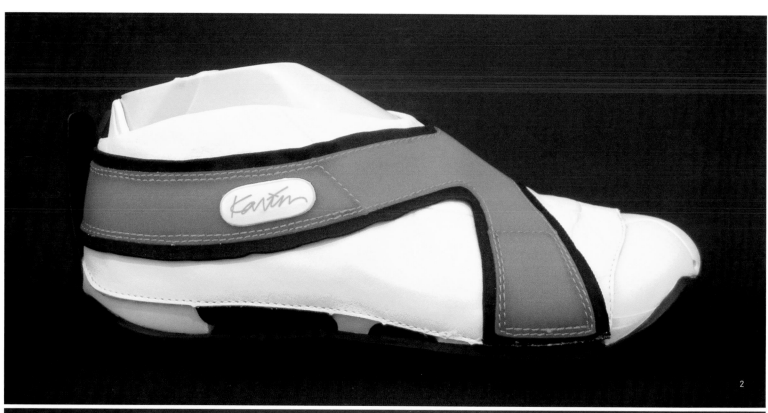

2

3

4

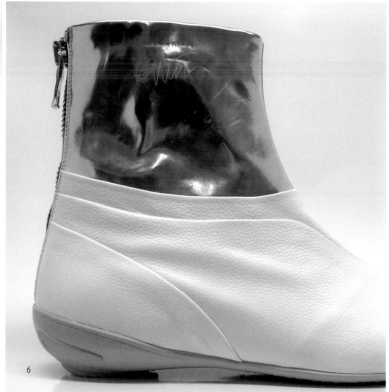

5

6

8

9

SRULI RECHT | REYKJAVIK, ICELAND

www.srulirecht.com

Photos © Sruli Recht

1　The Messengers Veins, Structured boot with cuff, burnt umber buffalo skin, 2008
2　With A Silvertongue, Transitional shoe with folding button down tongue to become motorcycle boot, hull pine heel, midnight brown goat skin, 2008
3　With A Silvertongue, Transitional shoe with folding button down tongue to become motorcycle boot, hull pine heel, gunmetal cow skin, 2008
4　With A Silvertongue, Transitional shoe with folding button down tongue to become motorcycle boot, hull pine heel, rust kangaroo skin, 2008
5　Grey Nurse, Button up pleated ankle boot with cuban heel, kelp green cow skin, 2008
6　Hvalsforhúðsskór - Dorks, Button up pleated ankle boot with cuban heel, caramel sandstone minke dork, 2008

Sruli Recht was born in Israel and educated in Australia, establishing his eponymous label in Reykjavik, Iceland. The footwear collection blends the craft of shoe making, draping and post-modernism. Using fascinating materials such as minke dork, kangaroo, pine, perch, and buffalo the end result mixes cyberpunk, artisan shoe making and sculptural construction.

In Israel geboren und in Australien ausgebildet, gründete Sruli Recht sein gleichnamiges Label im isländischen Reykjavík. Seine Schuhkollektion vereint Schuhmacherhandwerk, Faltenwurf und Postmoderne. Er verwendet faszinierende Materialien wie Zwergwal-Penis, Känguru, Kiefer, Barsch und Büffel. Das Ergebnis ist eine Mischung aus Cyberpunk, kunsthandwerklicher Schuhfertigung und plastischer Konstruktion.

Sruli Recht nació en Israel y cursó sus estudios en Australia antes de fundar su marca epónima en Reykjavik, Islandia. Su colección de calzado combina la fabricación artesanal de zapatos, las telas con pliegues y el postmodernismo. El diseñador aplica materiales tan fascinantes como el prepucio de ballena menor, la piel de canguro, el pino, la perca y el búfalo. El resultado es una mezcla de ciberpunk, artesanía del calzado y construcción escultórica.

Né en Israël et formé en Australie, Sruli Recht fonda son label éponyme à Reykjavik en Islande. Sa collection de chaussures conjugue artisanat de la chaussure, draperie et postmodernisme. Il utilise des matériaux fascinants tels que la peau de baleine, de kangourou, de perche, de bison et l'écorce de pin. Cela donne un mélange de cyberpunk, d'artisanat de chaussure et de construction sculpturale.

Nato in Israele, Sruli Recht studiò in Australia e fondò la sua omonima marca a Reykjavik, in Islanda. La sua collezione di scarpe è un connubio di artigianato, panneggio e postmodernismo. Utilizza materiali affascinanti quali prepuzio di balenottero, canguro, pino, cernia e bufalo; il risultato finale è un mix di fantascientifico stile punk, artigianato e costruzione plastica.

2

2

3

4

3

5

6

ROSA MOSA | VIENNA, AUSTRIA
Simone Springer, Yuji Mizobuchi

www.rosamosa.com

Photos © Martin Stoebich (1), Irina Gavrich (2, 7), Doris Erben (3, 4), Ruth Bayer (5), Wolfgang Thaler (6, 8)

1 beige / latte doubleface sheepskin sandal, rm collection SS 2008
2 image campaign, rm collection AW 2006 / 07
3 multicolor rag-woven / calf leather low-cut boot, rm collection AW 2007 / 08
4 multicolor rag-woven / calf leather cross-strap pump, rm collection AW 2008 / 09
5 soft cotton / goat skin pump with nutwood heel, rm collection AW 2007 / 08
6 shrunk cow hide zip up boots in latte / burly wood
7 deer skin / umbrella fabric pumps with natural rubber sole, rm collection AW 2006 / 07
8 beta and gamma, semi-dyed linden wood soled clogs with upper leather made from deer skin in white and black

Austrian born Simone Springer and Japanese born Yuji Mizobuchi are the designers behind Rosa Mosa. Focusing on three main aspects—material, shape and proportion—each of their products is created as an artist creates a sculpture. Collaborating with local Alpine tanneries and craftsmen they translate traditional shoe handicrafts into innovative and experimental designs infused with Japanese elements. Their different cultural backgrounds are often a recurring theme in their collections.

Die in Österreich geborene Simone Springer und der aus Japan stammende Yuji Mizobuchi sind die beiden Designer hinter dem Label Rosa Mosa. Im Mittelpunkt ihrer Arbeiten stehen die drei Aspekte Material, Form und Proportion; jedes ihrer Produkte wird so angefertigt wie ein Künstler eine Skulptur herstellt. In Zusammenarbeit mit lokalen Gerbereien in den Alpen und Handwerkern entstehen aus traditionellen, von Hand angefertigten Schuhen innovative und experimentelle Designs mit japanischem Touch. Ihre unterschiedliche kulturelle Herkunft ist ein häufig wiederkehrendes Thema in ihren Kollektionen.

Simone Springer, de origen austriaco, y Yuji Mizobuchi, de raíces japonesas, son las mentes creativas tras la marca Rosa Mosa. Sus diseños se sustentan en tres pilares básicos: el material, la forma y las proporciones. Estos diseñadores crean sus productos tal como un artista da forma a una escultura. El dúo coopera con curtidores de los Alpes y artesanos locales y traduce así la fabricación tradicional de calzado en diseños innovadores y experimentales con un toque japonés. El diferente origen cultural de estos dos diseñadores se refleja a menudo en sus colecciones.

L'autrichienne Simone Springer et le japonais Yuji Mizobuchi sont les créateurs de Rosa Mosa. Ils se concentrent sur trois aspects principaux : matériau, forme et proportion. Chacun de leurs produits est créé à la façon d'un artiste sculpteur. En coopération avec des tanneries locales dans les Alpes et des artisans d'art, ils transforment des chaussures traditionnelles faites à la main en designs expérimentaux imprégnés d'éléments japonais. Leurs différentes origines culturelles sont un sujet récurrent dans leurs collections.

L'austriaca Simone Springer e il giapponese Yuji Mizobuchi sono gli stilisti che stanno dietro la marca Rosa Mosa. Ciascuno dei loro articoli, tutti incentrati principalmente su tre aspetti (materiale, forma e proporzione), è realizzato nello stesso modo in cui un artista crea una scultura. In collaborazione con concerie e artigiani delle regioni alpine, i due designer trasformano modelli tradizionali realizzati a mano in creazioni innovative e sperimentali arricchite con qualche tocco d'influenza giapponese. Il loro diverso background culturale è spesso un tema ricorrente nelle loro collezioni.

3

4

7

OLIVER SWEENEY | DEVON, UK

www.oliversweeney.com

Photos © Oliver Sweeney

1 Route, updated two tone Brogue style in black and ivory with the new mustang toe shape, AW 2008
2 Race, cracked leather ankle boot in iccaro green with angular side zips, SS 2008
3 Plunge, new style Derby lace-up in the latest colourway (lima bordo) with the new mustang toe shape and a subtly distressed leather finish, AW 2008
4 Dave, hard wearing leather boot in tan with a rubber sole and practical side zips, AW 2008
5 Twister, classic and popular Brogue in black golf and ivory two tone leather, AW 2008

Leicester born Sweeney is a designer with a long history and experience of handmade shoes. His footwear is easily recognizable, with a combination of detail and construction that emphasises his strong design identity. The collections are made in Italy using traditional shoemaking techniques with added contemporary detailing.

Der in Leicester geborene Designer Oliver Sweeney kann eine überzeugende Biografie und viel Erfahrung im Bereich handgefertigter Schuhe sein eigen nennen. Seine Schuhe haben einen hohen Erkennungswert; eine starke Identität und eine Kombination von Details und Konstruktionen machen deutlich, dass es sich um seine Entwürfe handelt. Sweeneys Kollektionen werden in Italien gefertigt, wobei traditionelle und moderne Techniken der Schuhmacherei sich ergänzen.

En el repleto currículo del diseñador Oliver Sweeney, nacido en Leicester, destaca sobre todo su extensa experiencia en la fabricación artesanal de calzados. Sus creaciones son inconfundibles, con una marcada identidad y una combinación de detalles y construcciones que distinguen sus diseños de los de cualquier otro. Sus colecciones son confeccionadas en Italia aplicando técnicas de zapatería tradicional complementadas con procedimientos modernos.

Né à Leicester, Oliver Sweeney est un dessinateur doté d'un vécu impressionnant en matière de chaussures faites à la main. Facilement reconnaissables, ses souliers à l'identité forte sont dotés d'extras attestant que l'on porte bien son design. Les collections sont fabriquées en Italie grâce aux méthodes traditionnelles de la cordonnerie ainsi qu'aux techniques modernes.

Nato a Leicester, Sweeney è uno stilista con una lunga tradizione ed esperienza nel campo delle calzature realizzate a mano. Le sue creazioni sono facilmente riconoscibili per la loro forte identità e una combinazione di particolari e tecniche che fanno capire immediatamente di quale marca si tratta. Le calzature sono prodotte in Itala con l'impiego di tecniche tradizionali arricchite da dettagli in stile moderno.

3

4

MARLOES TEN BHÖMER | LONDON, UK

www.marloestenbhomer.com

Photos © Marloes ten Bhömer, Henri ter Hall (p 325)

1 Bluefoldedshoe, Leather and stainless steel, 2004
2 Fashion NL; The next generation, 2006: Foldedshoe, Wood and tarpaulin, 2001
3 Bluemâchéshoe, Leather and stainless steel, 2003
4 Redmâchéshoe, Stainless steel and leather, 2003
5 Carbonfibreshoe #2, Carbon fibre and leather, 2003
6 Noheelsshoe, Polyurethane resin, 2003
7 Mouldedleathershoe, Vegetable tanned leather and carbon fibre, 2003
8 Greymâchéshoe, Leather and stainless steel, 2005

Marloes Ten Bhömer is a Royal College of Art product design graduate. She has chosen footwear to be her product producing shoes that are both provocative and visionary. Ten Bhömer's passion for footwear is undisputed. Her creations inspire, explore new silhouettes and push the boundaries of design.

Marloes Ten Bhömer studierte Produktdesign am Royal College of Art und machte Schuhe zu ihrem Produkt. Diese kommen bei Ten Bhömer provokativ und visionär daher. Ihre Leidenschaft für Schuhe ist unbestritten; ihre Kreationen inspirieren, erforschen neue Silhouetten und verschieben die Grenzen des Designs.

Marloes Ten Bhömer cursó sus estudios de diseño en el Royal College of Art. Esta diseñadora se ha especializado en el calzado y sus creaciones son tan provocadoras como visionarias. Su pasión por los zapatos es innegable y su inspiradora obra explora nuevas formas y va más allá de los límites del diseño.

Issue du Royal College of Art où elle étudia le design de produit, Marloes Ten Bhömer choisit comme option les chaussures. Celles-ci se veulent à la fois provocatrices et visionnaires. La passion que Ten Bhömer voue aux chaussures est incontestée. Ses créations inspirent, explorent de nouvelles silhouettes et repoussent les limites du design.

Marloes Ten Bhömer studiò design presso il Royal College of Art specializzandosi in calzature, che la stilista confeziona con uno stile insieme provocatorio e visionario. La passione di Ten Bhömer per le scarpe è incontestata. Le sue creazioni stimolano la mente, esplorano nuove forme ed elevano il design a nuovi livelli.

2

3

4

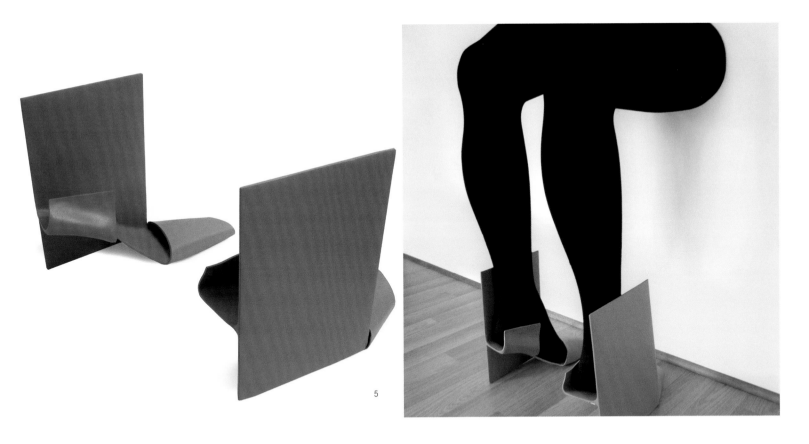

5

6

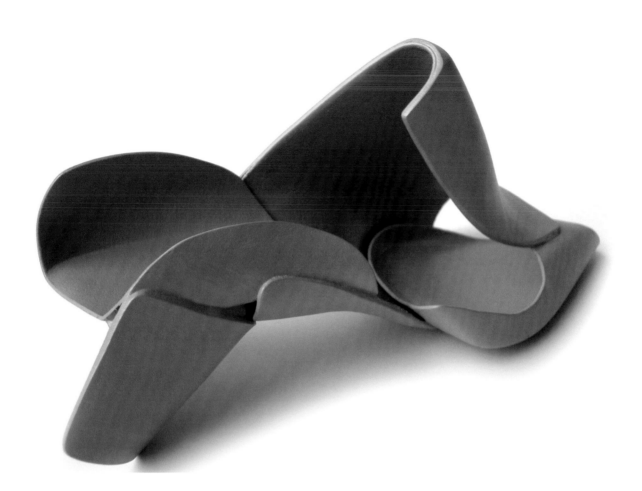

8

ANDREA TRAINA | FANO, ITALY

www.folets.com

Photos © Alessandro Brugnettini, James Frid (1), Christian Trippe (4)

1 Folets for AC, Vegetable Tanned Leather Shoe Box and Sandal, 2008
2 Red Vegetable Tanned Leather Shoe, 2007
3 Two-tone Vegetable Tanned Leather Boot, 2007 & Open Heel Vegetable Tanned Shoe, 2007
4 Folets for AC, Vegetable Tanned Leather Biker Boot, 2007
5 Group of Vegetable Tanner Leather Sandals, 2007

Andrea Traina is a master artisan who works solely by hand using medieval methods. All the shoes and leather goods are completely produced without the use of electricity. After a degree in the philosophy of physics, Traina has committed himself to a life of hand-crafted leather goods with products being noticed by fashion houses Kenzo and Antonio Marras.

Andrea Traina ist ein Meister des Kunsthandwerks. Er fertigt seine Modelle ausschließlich in Handarbeit an und bedient sich dabei mittelalterlicher Techniken. So werden alle Schuhe und Lederwaren ohne Zuhilfenahme von Strom hergestellt. Traina, der früher als Physiker arbeitete, hat sich einem Leben im Zeichen handgefertigter und fein bearbeiteter Lederwaren verschrieben. Seine Arbeiten rufen bei Modehäusern wie Kenzo oder Anotonio Marras großes Interesse hervor.

Andrea Traina es un maestro artesano que confecciona todas sus obras aplicando métodos medievales. Todos sus zapatos y artículos de cuero son producidos sin recurrir al uso de la electricidad. Tras licenciarse en Filosofía de la Física, Andrea Traina ha dedicado su vida a la marroquinería artesanal de alta calidad. Algunas firmas como Kenzo o Antonio Marras han sabido apreciar ya su trabajo.

Andrea Traina est un maître d'artisanat d'art qui confectionne ses modèles exclusivement à la main en se servant de méthodes médiévales. Toutes les chaussures et les articles en cuir sont fabriqués sans utiliser d'électricité. Titulaire d'un diplôme en physique théorique, Traina consacre sa vie aux produits faits à la main et fabriqués en cuir avec délicatesse suscitant ainsi l'intérêt de maisons de couture telles que Kenzo et Anotonio Marras.

Andrea Traina è un maestro artigiano che lavora esclusivamente a mano utilizzando metodi medievali. Tutte le scarpe e gli articoli in pelle sono confezionati senza fare ricorso all'elettricità. Dopo aver conseguito la laurea in fisica teorica, Traina si è dedicato interamente alla realizzazione a mano e alla rifinitura di articoli in pelle che oggi destano interesse in grandi case di moda quali Kenzo e Antonio Marras.

2

3

335

4

5

ZJEF VAN BEZOUW | AMSTERDAM, THE NETHERLANDS

www.zjefworks.com

Photos © Zjef Van Bezouw, Ton Werkhoven (5, 6)

1 Golden Boot, metallic leather with studs and aluminium coat hook heel, 2004
2 Ruffled Boot, leather with a heel made out of an aluminium coat hook, 2003
3 Dildo Boot, leather with a heel made from a metal dildo, 2003
4 Shiny Boot, patent leather with sole made from poured polyurethane, 1996
5 Dragon Boot, artificial printed leather with a removable tail at heel, 1993
6 Mirror Boots, leather with mirror foil inlays, 1992

Dutch designer Van Bezouw has created his shoe ideas around environments and performance. His shoes are one-off pieces with often provocative themes and ideas. The shoes are not made to follow any trends or fashions but are more for theatrical statement.

Der niederländische Designer Van Bezouw hat seine Schuhideen rund um die Aspekte Umgebung und Ausdruck angesiedelt. Seine Schuhe sind Einzelstücke mit oft provokativen Themen und Ideen. Die Schuhe sind nicht dazu da, Trends oder einer Mode zu folgen, sondern erfüllen vielmehr die Funktion eines theatralischen Statements.

Las creaciones del diseñador neerlandés de calzado Van Bezouw nacen a partir de su interpretación de entornos y expresiones. Sus zapatos son piezas únicas y a menudo muestran temáticas o ideas provocadoras. Bezouw no sigue tendencias o modas, sus creaciones cumplen más bien la función de una afirmación teatral.

Le dessinateur néerlandais Van Bezouw a créé ses idées de chaussures autour des notions d'environnement et d'expressivité. Ses souliers sont des fabrications hors série souvent enclines à la provocation. Les chaussures ne suivent pas de tendances ou de courants, elles ont plutôt une vocation théâtrale.

Lo stilista neerlandese Van Bezouw ha forgiato la propria idea di scarpe basandosi sui concetti di ambiente e performance. Le sue creazioni sono pezzi unici ispirati a temi e idee spesso provocatori. Non seguono mode o tendenze, ma sono piuttosto forme di espressione teatrale.

2

3

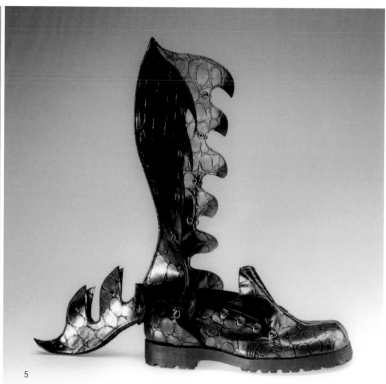

4

5

ATALANTA WELLER | LONDON, UK

www.atalantaweller.com

Photos © Christoph Bolten, Lauren Brown (portrait)

1   Boots, Atalanta Weller for House of Holland, Box Calf
    with Plaid, Autumn Winter 2008
2   Future shoes, wood and lacquer, 2007
3   Summer Wedge, Atalanta Weller for House of Holland,
    leather and hi gloss lacquer finish, Spring Summer 2008
4   Lace Shoes, Atalanta Weller for House of Holland, box
    calf with plaid, Autumn winter 2008

Atalanta studied at Cordwainers College, has worked for Clarks and Bruno Magli before successfully setting out on her own and most recently collaborating with Gareth Pugh and Henry Holland. Weller introduces new dimensions and extreme silhouettes into her ranges, with her designs being progressive and distinctly futuristic.

Atalanta Weller studierte am Cordwainers College, arbeitete für Clarks und Bruno Magli und geht nun sehr erfolgreich ihren eigenen Weg. Kürzlich kam es zu einer Zusammenarbeit mit Gareth Pugh und Henry Holland. Weller bringt neue Dimensionen und außergewöhnliche Silhouetten in ihre Produktpalette; ihre Designs sind progressiv und ausgesprochen futuristisch.

Atalanta cursó su carrera en el Cordwainers College y trabajó para Clarks y Bruno Magli antes de empezar su exitosa carrera como autónoma e iniciar su reciente colaboración con Gareth Pugh y Henry Holland. Weller introduce nuevas dimensiones e imposibles siluetas en sus líneas, marcadas por diseños progresivos y explícitamente futuristas.

Atalanta Weller fit ses études au Cordwainers College et travailla pour Clarks et Bruno Magli avant de suivre son propre chemin. A noter sa récente collaboration avec Gareth Pugh et Henry Holland. Weller enrichit sa gamme de nouvelles dimensions et de silhouettes poussées à l'extrême. Son design est progressif et résolument futuriste.

Atalanta studiò al Cordwainers College e lavorò per Clarks e Bruno Magli prima di iniziare la sua felice carriera da stilista autonoma e avviare, in tempi più recenti, la collaborazione con Gareth Pugh e Henry Holland. Le collezioni della Weller sorprendono per le nuove dimensioni e le forme estreme che propongono, che prendono forma in modelli progressisti e chiaramente futuristici.

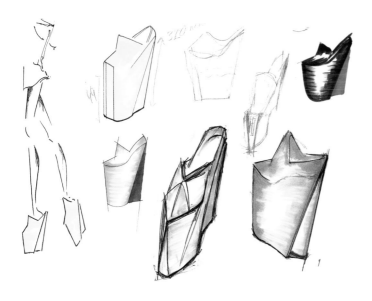

SASKIA WITTMER | FLORENCE, ITALY

saskiascarpesumisura@gmail.com

Photos © Federica Di Giovanni, Saskia Wittmer (p 353, 8), Martin Nink (portrait)

1 Francesina coda di rondine, english calf skin, 2002
2 Francesina giorno bi-color, kangaroo and suede skin, 2006
3 Stivaletto retro, box calf and suede, 2004
4 Mocassino, ostrish, 2007
5 Norwegese, english calf skin, 2001
6 Francesina sera, box calf and suede, 2007
7 Francesina coda di rondine, kangarooskin and linen, 2005
8 Light, suede, heel covered with mother of pearl, 2005

German born Saskia Wittmer is one of the few female made-to-measure men's shoe makers in the world. She has a studio and a shop in the heart of Florence where she focuses on the men's bespoke market. Her design and product introduces new elegant longer shapes to otherwise classical styles.

Die aus Deutschland stammende Saskia Wittmer gehört zu den wenigen Frauen des Schuhmacherhandwerks, die maßgeschneiderte Herrenschuhe fertigen. Sie besitzt ein Studio und einen Laden im Zentrum von Florenz, wo sie sich auf Maßschuhe für Herren spezialisiert hat. Ihr Design und Fabrikat bringen neue, elegante und längere Formen in die sonst klassisch orientierten Modelle.

La alemana Saskia Wittmer es una de las pocas artesanas en el mundo que realiza zapatos a medida para hombres. Wittmer, que posee un estudio y una tienda en el corazón de Florencia, se ha especializado en el mercado de la confección masculina personalizada. Sus diseños y productos sobreponen elegantes formas más estilizadas a los estilos clásicos.

Saskia Wittmer, d'origine allemande, est l'une des rares cordonnières de chaussures sur mesure pour hommes. Elle possède un studio et un magasin en plein cœur de Florence où elle se consacre aux souliers masculins faits sur mesure. Son design et produit apportent de nouvelles formes élégantes et plus longues à des modèles plutôt connus pour être classiques.

La tedesca Saskia Wittmer è una delle poche donne al mondo che disegnano calzature maschili su misura. Possiede uno studio e un negozio nel cuore di Firenze, dove la stilista si è specializzata nel confezionamento di scarpe maschili su ordinazione. Il suo design e le sue creazioni aggiungono forme nuove, più allungate ed eleganti, a modelli altrimenti classici.

2

8

ESTELLE YOMEDA | PARIS, FRANCE

www.estelleyomeda.com

Photos © Estelle Yomeda, Jacques Vekemans (1, 12, 13, portrait), Alexandre Callier (11)

1 Mesange, varnish leather and felt
2 Shelly, varnish leather with suede details
3 Franck, varnish leather and suede
4 Donna, varnish leather and nappa, shell heel
5 Lucy, varnish leather and suede, shell heel
6 Norma, nappa and varnish leather
7 Laura, nappa
8 Lucy, varnish leather and suede - shell heel
9 Donna, nappa and varnish leather - shell heel
10 Audrey, nappa and varnish leather - shell heel
11 Boudoir, suede and lace
12 Mika, varnish leather
13 Hibou, soft calf leather

Estelle Yomeda designs for and from her own unique world. Inspiration comes from being free and not tied down to seasonal trends with colour playing an important part in her poetic and feminine collections which are truly Parisian in spirit. Her individual looks have a selection of faithful followers such as Björk.

Estelle Yomeda entwirft für ihre und aus ihrer eigenen, einzigartigen Welt heraus. Aus dem Umstand frei und nicht auf saisonabhängige Trends festgelegt zu sein, zieht sie ihre Inspiration. Farben spielen in ihren poetischen und femininen, von echtem Pariser Esprit durchdrungenen Kollektionen eine große Rolle. Ihre individuellen Designs erfreuen sich treuer Fans, darunter auch Björk.

Estelle Yomeda diseña desde y para su particular mundo personal. Su inspiración se basa en la libertad de creación y la falta de compromiso con las tendencias de temporada. El juego con los colores constituye un elemento esencial en sus poéticas y femeninas colecciones, que encarnan el verdadero espíritu parisino. Sus individuales looks son admirados por un grupo de fieles seguidores, entre los que se encuentra Björk.

Estelle Yomeda conçoit pour son compte depuis le monde unique qui est le sien. Son inspiration lui vient de son indépendance vis-à-vis des tendances saisonnières. Les couleurs jouent un rôle important dans ses collections poétiques et féminines qui reflètent bien l'esprit parisien. Ses looks individuels font le bonheur de ses fidèles, parmi lesquels on trouve Björk.

Estelle Yomeda disegna per un mondo tutto suo ispirandosi a un mondo tutto suo. Le sue felici realizzazioni nascono dal suo essere completamente svincolata dalle tendenze stagionali. I colori svolgono un ruolo molto importante nelle sue collezioni, che riflettono il suo spirito parigino poetico e femminile. I suoi particolarissimi modelli vantano tutta una serie di fedeli ammiratori, tra i quali Björk.

2

3

4

5

8

9

10

11

12

RAPHAEL YOUNG | PARIS, FRANCE

www.monalisa-shoes.com

Photos © Manuele Geromini and Laura Villa Baroncelli

1 Edith, AW 2007
2 Amanda, AW 2007
3 Katarina, AW 2007
4 Suzanne, AW 2007
5 Rosalba, AW 2007
6 Jakie, AW 2007
7 Rina, AW 2007
8 Linda, AW 2007

Korean born Raphael Young grew up in France with an early obsession for shoes and their design. His collections have strong modern themes with elegant silhouettes and with a few seasons under his belt he is quickly becoming one of the most sought after designers.

Der in Korea geborene Raphael Young wuchs in Frankreich auf. Schon früh zeigte sich seine Leidenschaft für Schuhe und deren Design. Seine Kollektionen zeigen starke, moderne Themen und zeichnen sich durch elegante Silhouetten aus. Nunmehr seit mehreren Saisons tätig, ist er dabei, einer der gefragtesten Designer zu werden.

El diseñador Raphael Young de origen coreano creció en Francia y descubrió temprano su pasión por los zapatos y el diseño. Sus colecciones se caracterizan por sus marcados motivos modernos y elegantes formas. Tras unas pocas temporadas a sus espaldas, Young se está convirtiendo en uno de los diseñadores más solicitados del momento.

Né en Corée, Raphael Young a grandi en France. Très tôt, il montre un grand intérêt pour les chaussures et leur design. Ses collections se caractérisent par des thèmes forts et modernes avec des silhouettes élégantes. Ayant désormais plusieurs saisons à son actif, Young est en passe de devenir l'un des dessinateurs les plus prisés.

Il coreano Raphael Young è cresciuto in Francia maturando ben presto un'autentica passione per le scarpe e il loro design. Le sue collezioni sono caratterizzate da uno stile marcato e moderno e da una linea elegante. Con ormai diverse stagioni alle spalle, Raphael è destinato a diventare in breve tempo uno degli stilisti più richiesti in questo campo.

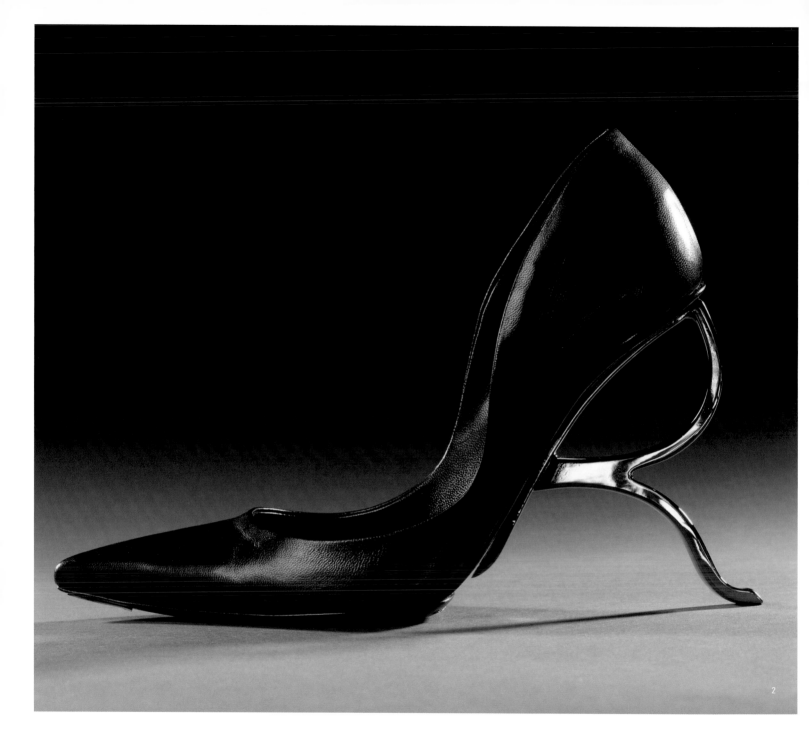

3

6

EDITORS

Aki Choklat is a footwear and accessories designer based in London, England. He runs his own label and lectures in various fashion and design schools throughout UK and Europe.

Aki Choklat lebt in London. Er designt Schuhe und Accessoires, hat sein eigenes Label und hält Vorlesungen in verschiedenen Mode- und Designschulen in Großbritannien und anderen europäischen Ländern.

Aki Choklat est dessinateur de chaussures et d'accessoires et vit à Londres. Il gère son propre label et donne des cours magistraux à plusieurs écoles de mode et de design au Royaume-Uni et dans d'autres pays européens.

Aki Choklat es un diseñador de calzado y accesorios residente en Londres. Además de dirigir su propia empresa, es profesor en diversas escuelas de moda y diseño británicas y europeas.

Aki Choklat è un designer di scarpe e accessori residente a Londra. Oltre a dirigere la propria azienda lavora come professore in diversi istituti di moda e design inglesi ed europei.

AKI CHOKLAT | LONDON, UK

www.akichoklat.com

Photos © Christian Trippe, Tessa Oksanen (portrait)

Rachel Jones is a footwear designer and trend forecaster based in London. She works as a global trend consultant and colour specialist working with leading footwear companies, and runs her own women's footwear brand.

Rachel Jones ist Schuhdesignerin und Trendscout und lebt in London. Sie arbeitet als allgemeine Trendberaterin und Farbspezialistin für führende Schuhunternehmen und leitet ihre eigene Damenschuhmarke.

Rachel Jones es una diseñadora de calzado y augur de tendencias afincada en Londres. Trabaja como asesora de moda global y especialista cromática para empresas punteras de calzado y dirige su propia marca de calzado femenino.

Rachel Jones est une dessinatrice de chaussures et une renifleuse de tendances qui a son activité à Londres. Elle travaille comme conseillère en tendances et spécialiste en couleurs pour des entreprises de chaussures leaders. En plus, elle est à la tête de sa propre marque de chaussures femme.

Rachel Jones è una designer di calzature e una cacciatrice di tendenze residente a Londra. Lavora come consulente di moda ed esperta di colori per importanti case produttrici di scarpe di tutto il mondo e dirige il proprio brand di calzature femminili.

RACHEL JONES | LONDON, UK

www.raejones.co.uk

Photos © Sandra Waibl, Gustavo Papaleo (portrait)

INDEX

© 2009 daab
cologne   london   new york

published and distributed worldwide by
daab gmbh
friesenstr. 50
d-50670 köln

p + 49 - 221 - 913 927 0
f   + 49 - 221 - 913 927 20

mail@daab-online.com
www.daab-online.com

publisher ralf daab

creative director feyyaz

editorial project by fusion publishing gmbh berlin
© 2009 fusion publishing, www.fusion-publishing.com

team
aki choklat (editor), rachel jones (co-editor)
katharina feuer, manuela roth (editorial coordination), rachel jones (text), simone bürger, manuela roth
(layout), jan hausberg (prepress + imaging), alphagriese (translations)

the editors would like to thank the following for their help in this project:
geordie diaz, claudio scalas, rebeca diaz, diane becker, heather blake, mark emmett, sarah keith,
deborah roberts, luca bianchini, melissa needham, david capon, stefan knight, ben jacobs

photo credits
coverphoto natacha marro, backcover emily hautier
introduction page 9 vicente esteban, 11 nina merikallio, 13 marloes ten bhömer,
15 richard james, 17 tessa oksanen

printed in germany
www.cantz.de

isbn 978-3-86654-050-7

all rights reserved.
no part of this publication may be reproduced in any manner.